Special thanks to the project underwriter:

BOEING

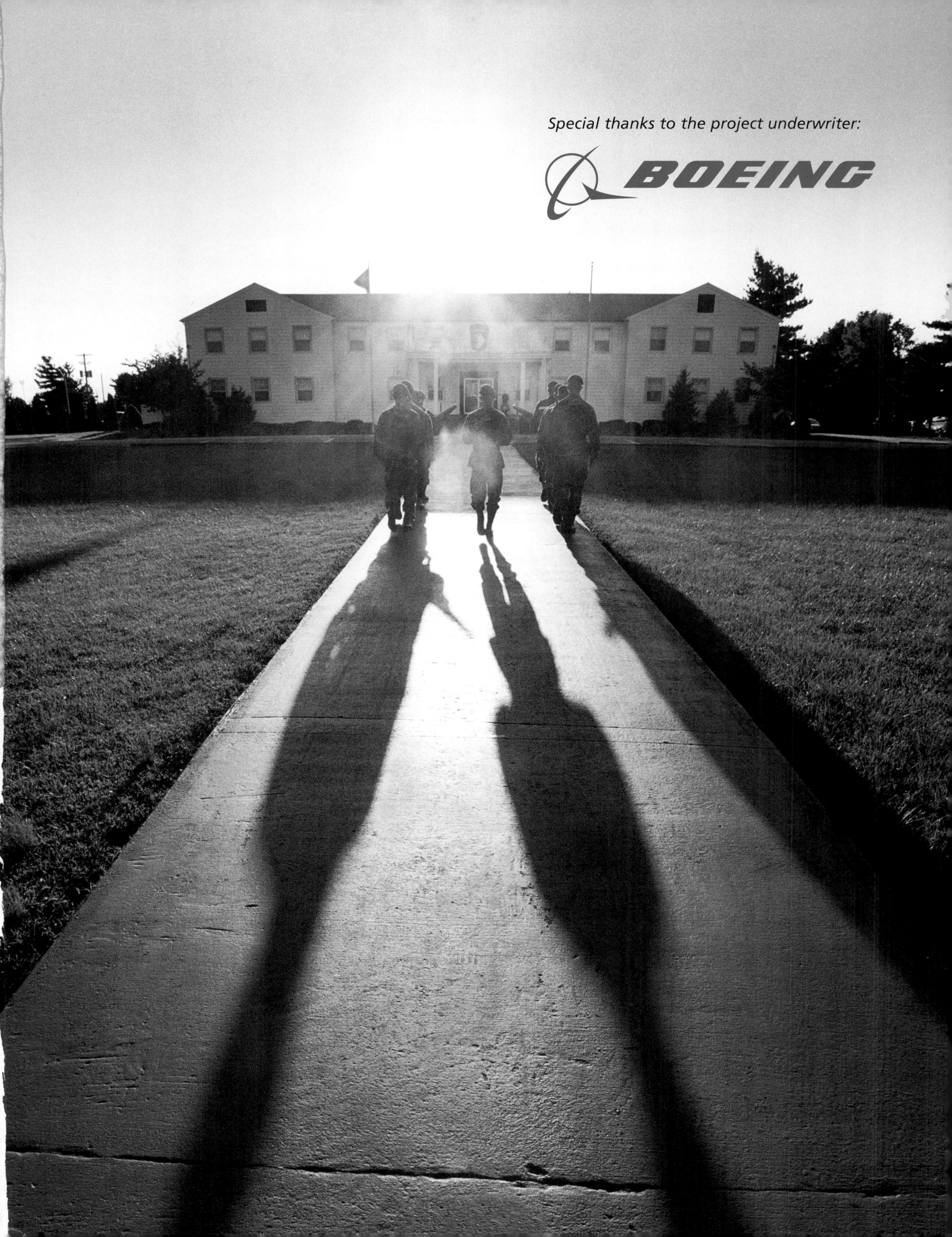

*This book is dedicated with deep gratitude
to the generations of brave Americans
who have served, are serving, and will serve
in the armed forces of their country.*

Previous page: Fort Campbell, Kentucky. *Photo by Dick Swanson*
This page: Twentynine Palms, California. *Photo by Les Stone*

Produced by Matthew Naythons and Lewis J. Korman
Editorial Director: Dawn Sheggeby
Director of Photography: Acey Harper
Creative Director: Tom Walker
Executive Producer: David Hume Kennerly

An EpiCom Media Book

www.daymilitary.com

Chairman: Lewis J. Korman
Co-Chairman: Robert Gottlieb
President and CEO: Matthew Naythons

HarperCollins*Publishers*

HarperCollins books may be purchased for educational, business, or sales
promotional use. For information, please write: Special Markets Department,
HarperCollins Publishers Inc., 10 East 53rd Street, New York, NY 10022.

"A Day in the Life of " is a trademark of HarperCollins Publishers Inc.
and is registered in the United States Patent and Trademark Office and
in other countries.

FIRST EDITION

Printed on acid-free paper

Library of Congress Cataloging-in-Publication Data is available upon request.

ISBN 0-06-054180-6

03 04 05 06 07 / 10 9 8 7 6 5 4 3 2

○ *Below*

Fort Polk, Louisiana—Soldiers near the end of a pre-dawn company run at Fort Polk, home of the Army's Joint Readiness Training Center, which provides unit training for light infantry forces. In recent years, soldiers from Fort Polk have served in operations Just Cause, Desert Storm, Restore Hope, Safe Haven, and Uphold Democracy.
Photo by David Gilkey

A B-2 stealth bomber readies for takeoff. Capable of traveling 6,000 miles without refueling, the B-2 has flown numerous nonstop missions to Afghanistan from its home base at Whiteman Air Force Base in Missouri.
Photo by Karen Ballard

A DAY IN THE LIFE OF
THE UNITED STATES
ARMED FORCES

Photographed by

125 of the world's leading photojournalists

on a single day, October 22, 2002

 Created by Matthew Naythons and Lewis J. Korman
An EpiCom Media Book

At Camp Tecson in the Philippines, an Army captain from the 1st Special Forces Group trains Philippine army rangers. As part of Operation Enduring Freedom, more than 1,200 American military personnel have been sent to train, advise, and assist their Filipino counterparts in fighting terrorism. *Photo by Robert McNeely*

The steam from a powerful jet-launching catapult drifts across the deck of the USS *Constellation*, shortly before the ship was deployed to the Persian Gulf from its home base in San Diego. *Photo by C. W. Griffin*

In Service to Our Country
by Walter Cronkite

Of all the military luminaries and historians you would expect to preface this timeless portrait of the American Armed Forces, I have a strong feeling that I was chosen for my picture. As you see, I'm shown wearing the uniform worn by American war correspondents for most of World War II.

When I was sent to war by the United Press News Service shortly after the bombing of Pearl Harbor, the military still hadn't decided on an appropriate uniform for correspondents who would—without even the suggestion of basic training—accompany the armed forces into combat. Finally, the decision was made that we would wear Army officers' uniforms without any insignia of rank or branch of service. To be easily identified, we were to wear around our left arms a green brassard bearing a large, white letter "C" for correspondent.

On my first assignment, aboard the battleship *Arkansas* escorting a convoy across the Atlantic, the naval officers took one look at the "C" and concluded that I was a chaplain. Equally bewildered British officers at a Scotland officers' club mistook it as a symbol of a cashiered officer and bridled at my audacity to be drinking at a gentlemen's bar.

To relieve such misunderstandings the military shortly replaced the "C" with shoulder patches bearing the unmistakable legend "War Correspondent." At the risk of overstating my military involvement or carrying on about what it was like in the old corps, the real Navy, or in the wild blue yonder, that patch on my uniform provided for me a box seat for observing and experiencing all branches of the service in combat over the past 60 years. Over this time, I have seen the American military change in character to more accurately reflect the racial, ethnic, and religious diversity of our vast country. I have seen all branches of the service welcome women into their ranks.

The book you hold, *A Day in the Life of the United States Armed Forces*, is their story. During the 24 hours of October 22, 2002, more than 125 of the finest photographers traveled the world to record the lives of the men and women in the military services. The common denominator in these revealing photographs is "service"—an ideal and an American tradition that is little changed throughout the years and between the branches. All of the world's technological advances have yet to replace the service tradition of a typical recruit's day, which usually begins with PT (physical training) at dawn and ends, well after dusk, within a few square feet of semi-private space where the recruit may be found quietly contemplating the day's accomplishments and the civilian life left behind.

In the service of their country, these Americans of all branches, ranks, and ethnic, religious, and socioeconomic backgrounds accomplish extraordinary tasks day in and day out, maintaining, training, and equipping themselves for combat readiness. *A Day in the Life of the United States Armed Forces* is a window into this world—the branches of which run quietly and without pause. Those who have left behind ordinary lives will, in future years, be spinning yarns that almost invariably will begin: "Now when I was in the service...." Such tales of service days, in the Dickensian pattern of "It was the best of times and the worst of times," will unfold, to breathe nostalgic life into moments that exemplified the extraordinary in the ordinary.

All of the men and women portrayed in this book are volunteer professionals in the Army, Navy, Air Force, Marines, and Coast Guard. Look at them closely and you will see representatives of every constituency of our society united, of their own volition, in a common mission. The devastating terrorist attacks of September 11, 2001, and the subsequent events may make it easier for civilians to comprehend and appreciate their dedication and the utter commitment to service that maintains and makes possible our freedoms.

This is a book of very few words, but it is not a quick read. I invite you to spend some time with these revealing photographs, to look beyond the uniforms, the camouflaged faces, and all the sophisticated tools of their trades. No matter your age, ethnicity, politics, or previous exposure to the armed forces, I trust that you will find this book to be a timeless primer on the fundamental selflessness, determination, and camaraderie that comes with the demands and honor of having served one's country, past and present.

The uniforms may change with the times and the military specialty, but never the dedication and contribution to our nation's welfare.

December 20, 2002
New York, New York

A Day with the U.S. Armed Forces

A *Day in the Life of the United States Armed Forces* **was conceived in the aftermath of September 11, 2001.** On that terrible morning, the complacency many of us had about the security of America vanished, and the need for a strong and vigilant military became more apparent.

We came to realize how little we really knew about the men and women of America's armed forces, a realization that was only heightened when news broadcasts began addressing the possibility of war with Iraq.

Who were they? Where were they stationed in America and around the world? How did they spend their time? What did it take to acquire the skills for their jobs? What motivated and inspired them?

We decided to find out, by looking beyond the headlines and taking a magnifying glass—"A Day in the Life"—to an ordinary day, October 22, 2002. Over the course of 24 hours, 125 of the world's best photographers aimed their cameras at the men and women of the U.S. Army, Air Force, Navy, Marine Corps, and Coast Guard. They followed them from midnight to midnight in the locations around the world, as shown on the accompanying maps.

More than 250,000 photographs were taken on that day. The 300 representative photographs that appear in this book are images of Americans—our sons, daughters, friends, and neighbors—who volunteer their lives to defend America's freedoms.

Matthew Naythons
Lewis J. Korman
Producers, *A Day in the Life of the*
United States Armed Forces

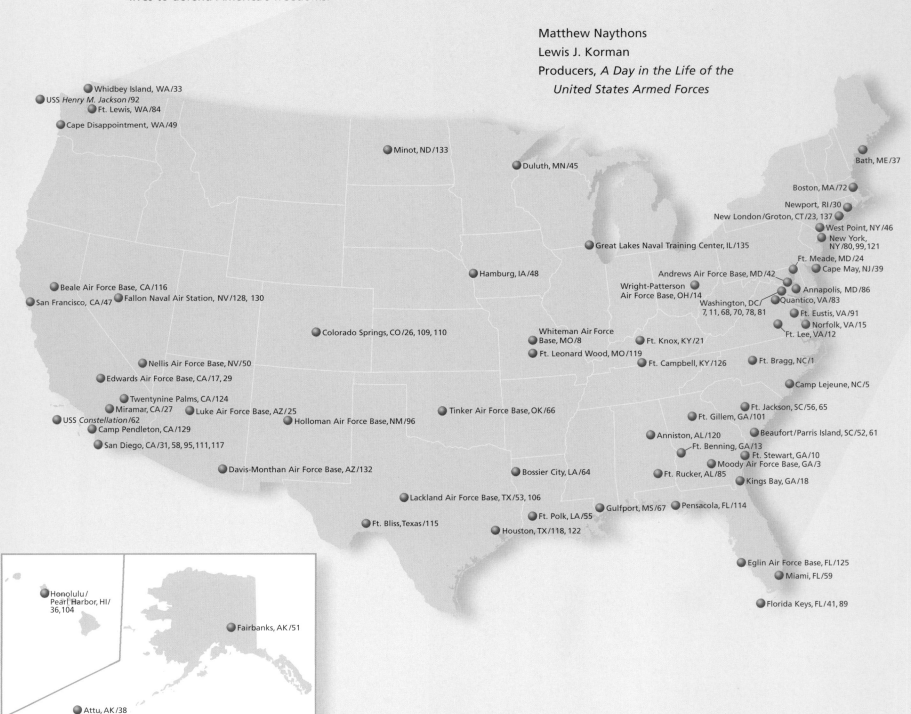

Whidbey Island, WA/33
USS *Henry M. Jackson*/92
Ft. Lewis, WA/84
Cape Disappointment, WA/49
Minot, ND/133
Duluth, MN/45
Bath, ME/37
Boston, MA/72
Newport, RI/30
New London/Groton, CT/23, 137
West Point, NY/46
New York, NY/80, 99, 121
Great Lakes Naval Training Center, IL/135
Ft. Meade, MD/24
Cape May, NJ/39
Hamburg, IA/48
Andrews Air Force Base, MD/42
Wright-Patterson Air Force Base, OH/14
Annapolis, MD/86
Beale Air Force Base, CA/116
Quantico, VA/83
San Francisco, CA/47
Fallon Naval Air Station, NV/128, 130
Washington, DC/ 7, 11, 68, 70, 78, 81
Ft. Eustis, VA/91
Norfolk, VA/15
Ft. Lee, VA/12
Colorado Springs, CO/26, 109, 110
Whiteman Air Force Base, MO/8
Ft. Knox, KY/21
Nellis Air Force Base, NV/50
Ft. Leonard Wood, MO/119
Ft. Bragg, NC/1
Edwards Air Force Base, CA/17, 29
Ft. Campbell, KY/126
Camp Lejeune, NC/5
Twentynine Palms, CA/124
Miramar, CA/27
Luke Air Force Base, AZ/25
Tinker Air Force Base, OK/66
Ft. Jackson, SC/56, 65
Ft. Gillem, GA/101
USS *Constellation*/62
Holloman Air Force Base, NM/96
Camp Pendleton, CA/129
Anniston, AL/120
Beaufort/Parris Island, SC/52, 61
San Diego, CA/31, 58, 95, 111, 117
Ft. Benning, GA/13
Ft. Stewart, GA/10
Moody Air Force Base, GA/3
Davis-Monthan Air Force Base, AZ/132
Bossier City, LA/64
Ft. Rucker, AL/85
Kings Bay, GA/18
Lackland Air Force Base, TX/53, 106
Gulfport, MS/67
Pensacola, FL/114
Ft. Polk, LA/55
Ft. Bliss, Texas/115
Houston, TX/118, 122
Eglin Air Force Base, FL/125
Miami, FL/59
Florida Keys, FL/41, 89
Honolulu/ Pearl Harbor, HI/ 36, 104
Fairbanks, AK/51
Attu, AK/38

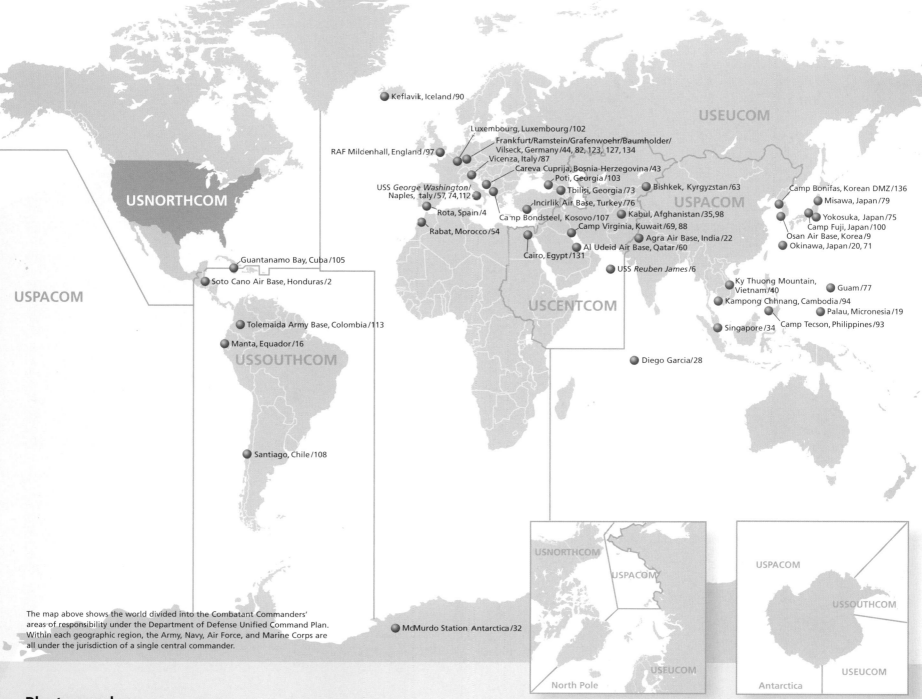

Keflavik, Iceland /90

Luxembourg, Luxembourg /102
Frankfurt/Ramstein/Grafenwoehr/Baumholder/
Vilseck, Germany /44, 82, 123, 127, 134
RAF Mildenhall, England /97
Vicenza, Italy /87
Careva Cuprija, Bosnia-Herzegovina /43
Poti, Georgia /103
USS George Washington/
Naples, Italy /57, 74, 112
Incirlik Air Base, Turkey /76
Rota, Spain /4
Camp Bondsteel, Kosovo /107
Rabat, Morocco /54
Camp Virginia, Kuwait /69, 88

Tbilisi, Georgia /73   Bishkek, Kyrgyzstan /63
Kabul, Afghanistan /35,98
Agra Air Base, India /22
Al Udeid Air Base, Qatar /60
Cairo, Egypt /131

Camp Bonifas, Korean DMZ /136
Misawa, Japan /79
Yokosuka, Japan /75
Camp Fuji, Japan /100
Osan Air Base, Korea /9
Okinawa, Japan /20, 71

USS Reuben James /6

USNORTHCOM

USPACOM

Guantanamo Bay, Cuba /105
Soto Cano Air Base, Honduras /2

Ky Thuong Mountain,
Vietnam /40   Guam /77
Kampong Chhnang, Cambodia /94
Singapore /34   Camp Tecson, Philippines /93
Palau, Micronesia /19

USCENTCOM

Tolemaida Army Base, Colombia /113

Manta, Equador /16

USSOUTHCOM

Diego Garcia /28

Santiago, Chile /108

USNORTHCOM
USPACOM
USEUCOM
North Pole

USPACOM
USSOUTHCOM
USEUCOM
Antarctica

McMurdo Station Antarctica /32

The map above shows the world divided into the Combatant Commanders'
areas of responsibility under the Department of Defense Unified Command Plan.
Within each geographic region, the Army, Navy, Air Force, and Marine Corps are
all under the jurisdiction of a single central commander.

Photographers

1. Eddie Adams
2. Lynsey Addario
3. Staff Sergeant Jeffrey Allen
4. Lieutenant Commander Scott Allen
5. Nancy Andrews
6. Photographer's Mate 1st Class Aaron Ansarov
7. Charlie Archambault
8. Karen Ballard
9. Photographer 1st Class Ted Banks
10. Anthony Barboza
11. Annie Griffiths Belt
12. Chief Journalist Robert Benson
13. P.F. Bentley
14. Erica Berger
15. Susan Biddle
16. Chief Petty Officer Johnny Bivera
17. Derk Blanset
18. Ira Block
19. Robin Bowman
20. Torin Boyd
21. Dudley M. Brooks
22. Christopher A. Brown
23. Honorary Coast Guard Auxiliarist Telfair H. Brown
24. David Burnett
25. Master Sergeant Michael C. Burns
26. David Butow

27. Chief Petty Officer Spike Call
28. Senior Airman Amanda Cervetti
29. Paul Chesley
30. Master Sergeant Lance S. Cheung
31. Carolyn Cole
32. Melanie Conner
33. Master Chief Photographer's Mate Terry A. Cosgrove
34. Michael Coyne
35. Sergeant Reeba Critser
36. Bruce Dale
37. Anne Day
38. Jesse Diamond
39. Al Diaz
40. Jay Dickman
41. David Doubilet
42. Eric Draper
43. Technical Sergeant Andy Dunaway
44. Lieutenant Colonel Michael Edgerington
45. Paul Fetters
46. John Ficara
47. Victor Fisher
48. Deanne Fitzmaurice
49. Petty Officer 1st Class Sarah Foster-Snell
50. Ruth Fremson
51. Rich Frishman
52. Paul Fusco
53. Alex Garcia

54. Liz Gilbert
55. David Gilkey
56. Technical Sergeant Efrain Gonzalez
57. Photographer's Mate Airman Konstandinos Goumenidis
58. Arthur Grace
59. Mark Greenberg
60. Stanley Greene
61. Lauren Greenfield
62. C. W. Griffin
63. Lori Grinker
64. Jack Gruber
65. Carol Guzy
66. Dirck Halstead
67. 1st Lieutenant Tana R. Hamilton
68. David Alan Harvey
69. Ron Haviv
70. Gregory Heisler
71. Gunnery Sergeant Matt Hevezi
72. Photographer's Mate Second Class Robert S. Houlihan
73. Nikolai Ignatiev
74. Photographer's Mate Airman Joan Elizabeth Jennings
75. Catherine Karnow
76. Ed Kashi
77. Nick Kelsh
78. David Hume Kennerly
79. Navy Journalist 1st Class Preston Keres
80. Staff Sergeant Gary Kieffer

81. Barbara Kinney
82. Douglas Kirkland
83. Andre Lambertson
84. Brian Lanker
85. Chang W. Lee
86. Sarah Leen
87. Barry Lewis
88. Staff Sergeant Bill Lisbon
89. Staff Sergeant Jeremy T. Lock
90. James Marshall
91. Photographer 1st Class Shane T. McCoy
92. Joe McNally
93. Bob McNeely
94. Dilip Mehta
95. Photographer's Mate 2nd Class Andrew Meyers
96. Genaro Molina
97. Seamus Murphy
98. Captain Chuck Mussi
99. Matthew Naythons
100. Robert Nickelsberg
101. Charles Ommanney
102. Paolo Pellegrin
103. Lucian Perkins
104. Mark Peterson
105. Larry C. Price
106. Technical Sergeant Justin D. Pyle
107. Master Sergeant Keith E. Reed
108. Alon Reininger

109. Mark Richards
110. Rick Rickman
111. Barbara Ries
112. Ricki Rosen
113. Raul Rubiera
114. Bob Sacha
115. Jeffrey Salter
116. Conrad Schmidt
117. Technical Sergeant Rick Sforza
118. Wally Skalij
119. Leif Skoogfors
120. Photographer's Mate 2nd Class Jennifer A. Smith
121. Petty Officer 1st Class Tom Sperduto
122. Ann States
123. Tom Stoddart
124. Les Stone
125. Jim Sugar
126. Dick Swanson
127. Guy Tillim
128. David Turnley
129. Peter Turnley
130. Commander Thomas R. Twomey
131. Ami Vitale
132. C.J. Walker
133. Clarence Williams
134. Corporal Eric L. Wilson
135. Donald R. Winslow
136. Michael Yamashita
137. Taro Yamasaki

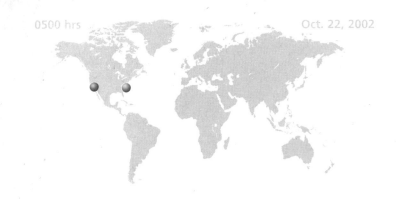

● *Above*

Coronado, California—His late-night, six-hour watch finally over, Aviation Structural Mechanic 3rd Class Sean Miller hunkers down for an early breakfast at the Night & Day Café, the only 24-hour diner near the Naval Air Station North Island near San Diego.
Photo by Photographers Mate 2nd Class Andrew Meyers

● *Right*

Fort Jackson, South Carolina—"Once I'm up and running," says Sergeant Thomas Gray, "caffeine is the priority of the day." No wonder. Gray, an Army drill instructor at Fort Jackson, begins his morning at 4 A.M. After a full day at the base—including PT, marching drills, and the inevitable paperwork—Gray finally hits the sack around midnight.
Photo by Carol Guzy

● **Top**

Fort Lewis, Washington—
First Platoon "Hellraisers"
perform their morning
physical training—pull-ups
and flutter kicks—under
the direction of Army Staff
Sergeant Jesus Negron. "These
are active-duty soldiers,"
says Negron, "and they're in
tip-top shape." PT starts at
6:30 A.M. and goes to 7:30,
sometimes 8:00 A.M.
Photo by Brian Lanker

● **Above**

Okinawa, Japan—Marines
wake up to the obstacle
course at Camp Kinser, just
a few feet from the shore
of the East China Sea. "It's
a beautiful place," says
photographer Torin Boyd.
"But for me it was way too
early for all that grunting
and groaning."
Photo by Torin Boyd

● *Above*

Washington, D.C.—"I started commuting this way because the river was between me and the office," explains Chief Master Sergeant David Power, "and then I decided to have some fun with it." Power lives in Washington, D.C., and manages Air National Guard para-rescue operations from an office in Crystal City, Virginia. Once only a fair-weather paddler, Power committed last year to kayaking across the Potomac year-round to raise scholarship money for the children of Special Operations soldiers, sailors, and airmen killed in action.
Photo by David Alan Harvey

● *Right*

Washington, D.C.—At 6:22 A.M., Secretary of Defense Donald Rumsfeld is already hard at work en route to the Pentagon. Rumsfeld is driven by security personnel and receives a daily news briefing, which he absorbs on his 20-minute ride to the office.
Photo by David Hume Kennerly

● *Right*

Keflavik, Iceland—War games begin before dawn on the desolate lava fields outside Keflavik. Lance Corporal Benjamin Baumann, 19, of Thibodaux, Louisiana, advances with his Marine platoon, based at the nearby naval air station. The Keflavik base has been in operation since the battle for the North Atlantic during World War II. "Training like this is sobering," says Baumann. "It brings the whole world situation into reality."
Photo by James Marshall

● *Above*

Yokosuka, Japan—In her 42nd year, the carrier USS *Kitty Hawk* is older than most of the 2,800 sailors who serve on board. Operating from Yokosuka, 65 miles south of Tokyo, the *Kitty Hawk* is the Navy's only permanently forward-deployed carrier. U.S. Pacific Fleet head-quarters in Pearl Harbor is 4,000 miles away.
Photo by Catherine Karnow

● *Right*

Boston Harbor, Massachusetts—Little Brewster Island is home to the Boston Light, the oldest operational Coast Guard lighthouse in the continental United States and the last with a full-time crew. Pairs of keepers spend ten days on the island, then take five days off. "During the week, I'm a manager for a boiler company," says Captain Ed Petrie (*right*) of the U.S. Coast Guard Auxiliary, who fills in as relief crew. In addition to maintaining the light, reporting the weather, and watching for boaters in distress, keepers' duties include caring for Sam and Cyrus, two black Lab mascots.
Photo by Photographer's Mate 2nd Class Robert S. Houlihan

● *Left*

Arlington, Virginia—Day breaks over the Tomb of the Unknown Soldier at Arlington National Cemetery. An Army honor guard patrols the area around the white marble sarcophagus, which holds the remains of an unknown American killed in World War I. Nearby, other crypts honor veterans of World War II, Korea, and Vietnam. On the back of this tomb is the inscription: "Here rests in honored glory an American soldier known but to God."
Photo by Annie Griffiths Belt

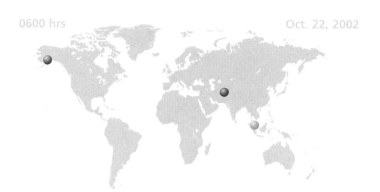

● **Top**

Bishkek, Kyrgyzstan—
Waking up in the tent she shares with two other women at Ganci Air Base, Air Force Staff Sergeant Kenisea Wiley of Boca Raton, Florida, enjoys a few extra moments of rest on her day off. The year-old U.S. Air Force station maintains and refuels combat and transport aircraft.
Photo by Lori Grinker

● **Above**

Fairbanks, Alaska—Staff Sergeant Patrick McDonald, a native of Beaufort, South Carolina, practices cold-weather survival techniques at the Army's Northern Warfare Training Center.
Photo by Rich Frishman

● *Below*

Singapore—Navy Postal Clerk 1st Class Charles Wilson, of Baton Rouge, Louisiana, plays "airplane" with his 2-year-old son, Matthew. Attached to a special unit that forwards ships' mail, Wilson lives in a black-and-white bungalow built by the British after World War II. "Before September 11, 2001, being stationed on shore was like having a 9 to 5 job," says Petty Officer Todd MacDonald, also based in Singapore. "It didn't feel like you were in the military, other than wearing your uniform at work. But since 9/11, things have changed, and the free time is pretty much gone. But there is no complaining—that's why we joined the military: to protect our country." ***Photo by Michael Coyne***

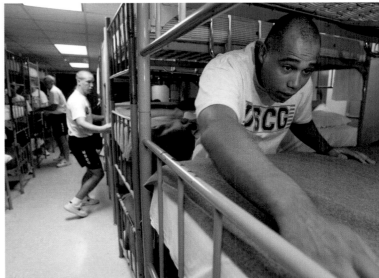

● *Top and above*

Cape May, New Jersey—
Seaman recruits line up, or
"muster," for roll call at 0530
hours at the U.S. Coast Guard
Training Center (*top*). Moments
later, recruit Johnny Jacobs
(*above*) hurries to "make his
rack." Between roll call and
breakfast, recruits have only
15 minutes to straighten their
bunks, shave, brush their
teeth, get dressed, and pack
their backpacks. "This being
boot camp," says Chief
Quartermaster Vaughan
Sutton, the normal penalty for
being late "is something
along the lines of push-ups."
Jacobs and the rest of L-163
Company graduated basic
training on December 7, 2002.
Photos by Al Diaz

Camp Virginia, Kuwait— Army Major Mark Weiner (at left) and Warrant Officer Dwayne Howell wash up after morning PT at Camp Virginia, a forward-support base less than 50 miles from the Iraqi border. It is one of five bases in Kuwait named after the states that suffered the most casualties in the terrorist attacks on September 11, 2001: New York, Virginia, Pennsylvania, Connecticut, and New Jersey.
Photo by Ron Haviv

🔵 *Top*

Kampong Chhnang, Cambodia—A bucket of cold water serves as a shower for Army Sergeant David Friedberg, a Boston native serving with the Cambodian Mine Action Center. Friedberg and a dozen Army colleagues teach first aid and trauma medicine to local medics.
Photo by Dilip Mehta

🔵 *Above*

Yokosuka, Japan—Just after sunrise, Electrician's Mate 2nd Class Uson Lewellyn enjoys coffee and a cigarette on the deck of Navy tugboat 787, the *Kittanning*, ported at Yokosuka.
Photo by Catherine Karnow

Vilseck, Germany—Two-year-old Samuel Edwards holds onto his dad, Sergeant 1st Class Norman Edwards, at the Vilseck Army Base. Edwards and his wife, Sergeant 1st Class Benita Edwards, are stationed there together. "Soldiers miss a lot of precious moments during their children's development because of the sacrifices in this line of business," Norman Edwards says. "We can both be called upon at any time, and having to uproot the children can cause confusion. But NCOs are taught to be proactive, whatever the mission. Make it happen."
Photo by Corporal Eric Wilson

● *Top*

Camp Bonifas, Korean DMZ—Between North and South Korea in the Demilitarized Zone, Army 1st Lieutenant James L. "Jack" Gleason of the U.N. Command Security Force starts his day in the lieutenants' barracks. His unit's motto: In Front of Them All.
Photo by Michael Yamashita

● *Above*

Nellis Air Force Base, Nevada—"Putting on my makeup in the car makes me the same as most women who aren't in the military," says Staff Sergeant Teresa Ulring, a paralegal at the base. "A mother with a full-time job juggles a lot in a small amount of time."
Photo by Ruth Fremson

🔘 **Right**

Fort Leonard Wood, Missouri—"I thoroughly enjoy having my family here," says Army Staff Sergeant Robert Parrish, standing with his wife, Edye, daughters, Megan and Jessica, and the family dog, Tucker, outside their post home at Fort Leonard Wood. "It keeps me motivated in my job, knowing my family is there for me when I get home."
Photo by Leif Skoogfors

🔘 *Top*

Misawa, Japan—Scripture comes with breakfast for the family of Major Court Wilkins, at Misawa Air Base. Originally from Bountiful, Utah, Wilkins is an optometrist at the base hospital.
Photo by Journalist 1st Class Preston Keres

🔘 *Above*

Eglin Air Force Base, Florida—"We think the Pledge is a good idea for our children," says Master Sergeant Donald Koser, whose family gathers to say the Pledge of Allegiance every morning in their home on the base. "It instills a sense of pride in the flag, pride in the nation, and a sense of duty to the country." Photographer Jim Sugar was impressed. "I've done a lot of military stories, and I understand what it is to be gung-ho patriotic. But this is patriotism of a different sort. It's personal, quiet, intimate, and very deeply felt."
Photo by Jim Sugar

● **Top**

Beaufort, South Carolina—
A future aviator heads to day care with his mother at the Beaufort Marine Corps Air Station, known to Marines as Fightertown, U.S.A.
Photo by Paul Fusco

● **Above**

San Diego, California—
Before going to work as a damage-controlman on the destroyer USS *Lassen,* Petty Officer 2nd Class Michael Barnett drops off 2-year-old son, Michael, at a San Diego Naval Station day-care center.
Photo by Carolyn Cole

● *Below*

Guantanamo Bay, Cuba— With help from her pint-sized personal trainer—1-year-old daughter Annette—Melissa Belleman grinds out pull-ups in 100-degree heat at the Guantanamo Bay Naval Base. Belleman, who is married to a Marine officer, is one of 850 Navy spouses, children, and other civilians living on the self-sufficient base, located 400 air miles southeast of Miami. ***Photo by Larry Price***

Major Dad

Photographs by Genaro Molina

My 6–year-old has a standing order for pancakes," says Air Force Major Lewis Wyatt. "But the other kids always want oatmeal or eggs or something else. Today, they get what Dad makes."

And today, the winner is…pancakes, per daughter Hanna's request, hot off the griddle in the kitchen of the Wyatt's five-bedroom house in Alamogordo, New Mexico. The house is about 15 miles from Holloman Air Force Base, where Wyatt flies F-117A stealth fighters as part of the 9th Fighter Squadron "Flying Knights." But before he goes to work, Wyatt likes to do what he calls "duty chores" around the house, and one of them is making breakfast for his wife, Kelly, and their eight children, ages 16 months to 16 years. As for the pancakes—"I make them from scratch," he says. "No mix."

For the Wyatt family, this stop is the sixth in the 19 years Lewis has been in the Air Force. And they expect to do it again, frequent moves from base to base

Left and top: *Air Force Major Lewis Wyatt makes breakfast for his eight children.* Above: *Wyatt and family in the backyard of their home near Holloman Air Force Base.*

being a part of military life. "The older kids have never known anything else," he says. "Military kids learn how to adjust. They arrive in a new place, and they go out and see what's happening and they make new friends." In fact, Wyatt and his family have only been separated three times, and that was during his deployment to the Middle East in the 1990s. About future separations he says: "There are no guarantees."

Wyatt's training flights on the F-117A usually last two hours, but there is a long debriefing after each flight, and only then does he get to drive home. Then it's dinner and quality time with his family, which can include playing games and

making music together. Does Wyatt find it difficult switching gears from being a fighter pilot to being an at-home dad? "Not really," he says. "Pilots learn to compartmentalize. When I'm flying, I'm thinking of nothing else. When I'm home, I like playing with my kids."

But true to a fighter pilot's spirit, Wyatt sees a competitive streak coming out in his kids, especially 6-year-old Hanna, the pancake queen. "She wants me to teach her how to play chess," he says, "and she hates to lose. I'm better than most of my kids right now, but that won't last for long."

Right: *At work at Holloman Air Force Base, Major Wyatt pilots an F-117A stealth fighter.* Top: *An impromptu jam session with 16-year-old son Sam and visiting father-in-law Bill Lehart.* Above: *An evening at home for Wyatt includes games with daughter Margaret, 8, and youngest son, Silas.*

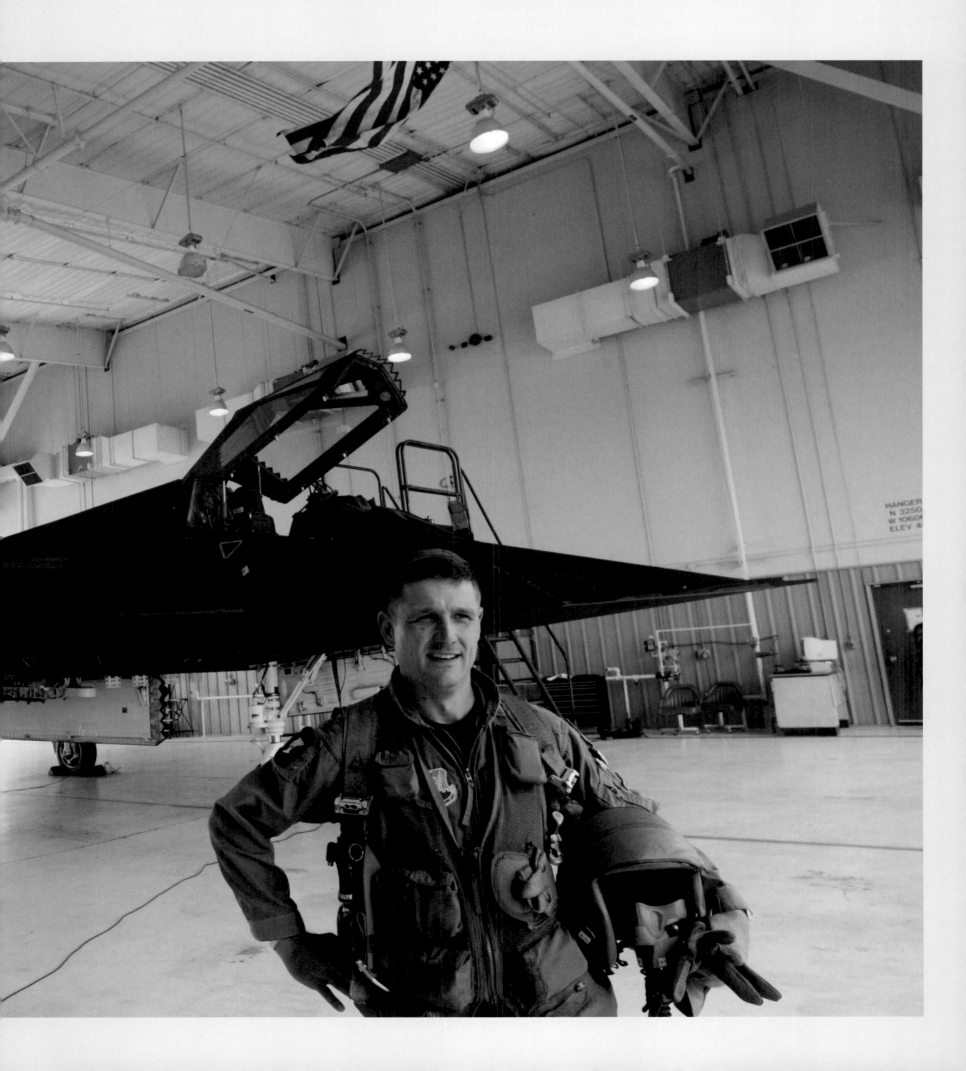

Kabul, Afghanistan—Breakfast on a tray is a welcome innovation for Army Specialist Eric Cabral, on guard duty at the Kabul Military Training Center in Afghanistan. The "tray pack," a new system of packaging and serving food in the field that includes more fresh and nutritious ingredients, is one of many recent improvements from the Defense Department's Combat Feeding Program. MREs—the notorious prepacked Meals Ready to Eat field rations—also got a major upgrade in 2002. Now it's Thai chicken and trendy pocket sandwiches, instead of mystery-meat casseroles and the frankfurters known in the Marine Corps as the Four Fingers of Death. Says Gerry Darsch, the program's director: "We store, distribute, and serve our foods from minus 60 up to 120 degrees. We also throw our stuff out of aircraft. Your local supermarket—I don't think—does that."
Photo by Captain Chuck Mussi

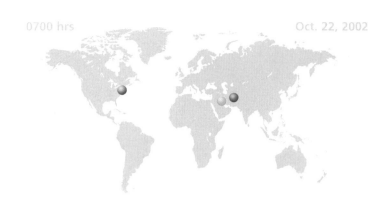

● *Top and following pages*

Cape May, New Jersey—
Recruits face the chow line at
the Coast Guard's training
center. As part of the rigors
of their 17-hour day, recruits
are required to eat breakfast
in silence and always appear
clean-shaven—even if that
means shaving twice or even
three times a day.
Photos by Al Diaz

● *Above*

Camp Virginia, Kuwait—
Army Private 1st Class
Kimberly Knight and her
husband, Private 1st Class Eric
Knight, share breakfast at
Camp Virginia. The couple
met at Fort Stewart, Georgia,
and were married over the
summer before deploying to
the Middle East.
Photo by Ron Haviv

Fort Benning, Georgia—Drill instructors comb through arriving Army recruits' personal effects for "contraband"— drugs and alcohol, weapons, food, tobacco products, and any non-religious reading material.
Photo by P. F. Bentley

● *Top and above*

Great Lakes Naval Training Center, Illinois—Navy recruits leave the trappings of civilian life behind. The first step for Anthony Amador of Kennedy, Texas, is saying goodbye to his long red locks (*top*). Recruits then get acquainted with their new gear, holding up each item and shouting its name to a drill instructor's cue (*above*).

The uniform boxes, handed out when recruits arrive, contain everything they will be allowed to use for the next nine weeks: shoes, underwear, toiletry items, a set of sweats, and the Navy's *Bluejacket's Manual*. All personal possessions are either mailed home or donated to a local charity.
Photos by Donald R. Winslow

Back to Boot Camp

Photographs by Arthur Grace

On October 22, 2002, photographer Arthur Grace, a former Marine lance corporal, revisited boot camp at the Marine Corps Recruit Depot in San Diego.

The last time I saw the inside of boot camp was at Parris Island, South Carolina, in August 1967. Things sure looked different in San Diego.

First of all, the kids today are volunteers—they want to be Marines, and they want to be good Marines. They know what they're getting into, so most of them arrive in reasonably good shape. The ones looking for brownie points

showed up with their hair already in a buzz cut.

The shock of where they are first hits them when they pile off the bus the first night, with the drill instructors screaming at them to line up on the yellow footprints. The adrenaline is rushing and everybody is racing around trying to do the right thing. Back on my bus in 1967, just about everyone there wanted to be a million miles away. One guy was so drunk, staggering around, that he couldn't even find the yellow footprints. You're not going to see that in 2002 at San Diego.

Once they get to the base they're not allowed to sleep until the next evening. They read the Uniform Code of Military Justice, which is painted on a wall. They go inside and empty their pockets, and then it's the haircut—the barber's been doing it for 30 years. They get their uniforms—basic fatigues, tennis shoes, T-shirts, skivvies. You yell out your size and they throw them at you. Next it's administrative stuff—lectures, issuing IDs, that sort of thing, all through the night. And then after some waiting around, it's morning, and they get some breakfast.

There are blood tests, hearing and vision tests. A dentist takes a look. Then you go to the barracks and learn to make your rack.

The purpose of boot camp is to strip away your civilian persona and replace it with a military persona. It's stress, stress, stress, and then they see how you handle it. They yell at you for not

Left and top: *New recruits arrive at the Marine Corps Recruit Depot in San Diego on the evening of October 22, 2002, beginning an all-night check-in process that will keep them up until Taps the following night.* Above: *Recruit Kyle Ochoa braves a contraband search.*

standing at attention, for not holding your cup with two hands, if your eyes aren't facing straight forward. I was amazed at how many hoarse drill instructors there were. Some guys actually blow out their vocal cords. In my day they could whack you to get your attention.

Now all they can do is yell a lot louder and a lot more. That plus push-ups, sit-ups, running in place, squat thrusts, for every and any infraction.

But I also had no idea how hard these drill instructors work—it's pretty much full-time from the day they pick up their platoons to the day their recruits graduate. I saw one kid who said he wanted to go home, that he'd made a terrible mistake. Three sergeants jumped in his face, yelling and screaming, "You can't leave! You think you can just leave?" Whatever it took to get him through the shock of one day being a civilian and the next having his head shaved and being just a guy in a uniform with a name tag and a number.

At the end of the day, while we were waiting for another bus to arrive, I was talking to a couple of drill instructors and they were teasing each other about who went through basic at San Diego—"the country club"—and who went through Parris Island. I asked one of the Parris Island guys, "What months?" He said January and February. I told him that he had it easy—I was there June through August, when it was 100 degrees and 100 percent humidity every day. He started laughing and asked me when I was there. I told him 1967, and he said, "Oh my God, are you old!" Both guys looked at me like I was from another planet. Today a Gulf War service ribbon makes you a veteran. Vietnam is ancient history to them.

Left: *Staff Sergeant Charles A. Joseph provides extra incentive to a focused recruit.* Top and above: *The first day of PT at San Diego's Marine Corps Recruit Depot takes its toll on the newcomers.*

● *Above and right*

Fort Jackson, South Carolina— Recruits wait their turn to negotiate the Victory Tower Complex, part of the obstacle course at the Army's Fort Jackson. The first phase of basic training is designed to boost confidence and instill a sense of teamwork, and includes training in physical fitness, drill and ceremony, basic first aid, map reading, and the military justice system. After passing a knowledge and skills test, recruits get their first chance to fire an M-16A2 rifle. ***Photos by Technical Sergeant Efrain Gonzalez***

Vicenza, Italy—Three times a week, Army MPs (military police) from the Southern European Task Force (SETAF) run to the church of Monte Berico, on a hilltop two and a half miles from the base at Vicenza.
Photo by Barry Lewis

● *Top*

Baumholder, Germany—
Army Staff Sergeant Rob E.
Bailey III grins and bears it
during a morning PT session.
An MP assigned to the 222nd
Base Support Battalion,
Bailey is also the assistant
coach of the Baumholder
American High School
football team.
Photo by Guy Tillim

● *Above*

Camp Bonifas, Korean DMZ—
"The world's most dangerous
golf course" is a single hole
and fairway surrounded by
bunkers, watchtowers,
barbed-wire fences, and land
mines at Camp Bonifas in
Korea's Demilitarized Zone.
Every morning, U.S. troops
attached to the U.N.
Command Security Force
run station drills on the
course's grass.
Photo by Michael Yamashita

● Left

Great Lakes Naval Training Center, Illinois—Navy recruits get a short breather during Battle Stations—an all-night drill that simulates conditions on a ship under fire. The exercise involves fighting through simulated fires in a smoke-filled room, jumping from a ship to a life raft, and carrying litters of "injured" personnel through the darkness amid mock explosions. The capstone event of Navy boot camp, Battle Stations is followed by a completion ceremony and a celebratory meal.
Photo by Donald R. Winslow

● Above

San Diego, California—Fifteen feet above the water's surface, Staff Sergeant Shawn D. Johnston teaches recruits how to position their bodies should they fall from any height into water. The exercise is just one facet of the water survival course at San Diego's Marine Corps Recruit Depot.
Photo by Arthur Grace

● Following pages

Parris Island, South Carolina—Women at the Marines' Parris Island training depot must learn to swim in full battle gear, which includes a 40-pound pack, helmet, and M-16 rifle. The exercise is called Combat Swim.
Photo by Lauren Greenfield

The Sarge

He is every raw recruit's nightmare—a loud, hectoring, sometimes foul-mouthed presence who gets you up at the crack of dawn, runs you ragged all day long and then demands that you go to sleep on the dot, on command, on his command. He is the drill sergeant, and boot camp just wouldn't be the same without him.

Photo by Carol Guzy

Drill sergeants were not formally part of the military until 1964, when, after a long study, the Army decided that recruits were not getting proper training. In 1972, female drill sergeants joined the ranks, and the only difference these days besides their gender, is their hats. Now there are drill sergeants (some are called drill instructors) in every branch of the military.

There is a good reason for the drill sergeant: If you can survive him or her, you can survive anything, and that's bad news for the enemy. This is the Army Drill Sergeant's Creed:

I am a Drill Sergeant.

I will assist each individual in their efforts to become a highly motivated, well disciplined, physically and mentally fit soldier, capable of defeating any enemy on today's modern battlefield.

I will instill pride in all I train. Pride in self, in the Army, and in country.

I will insist that each soldier meets and maintains the Army standards of military bearing and courtesy, consistent with the highest traditions of the U.S. Army.

Photo by Carol Guzy

I will lead by example, never requiring a soldier to attempt any task I would not do myself.

But first, last, and always, I am an American Soldier. Sworn to defend the Constitution of the United States against all enemies, both foreign and domestic.

I am a Drill Sergeant.

Top and above: *Staff Sergeant Angela Andrews and Staff Sergeant Thomas Gray break in new Army recruits at Fort Jackson, South Carolina.* Right: *Chief Quartermaster Vaughan Sutton at the Coast Guard Training Center in Cape May, New Jersey.*

Lackland Air Force Base, Texas—Vertical push-ups, eating bugs, and charming snakes are all part of Survival, Evasion, Resistance, and Escape training—SERE, for short. During the course, flight crews learn how to build temporary shelter, trap wild animals for food, and literally live off the land. To help them overcome their fear of snakes, trainees get acquainted with them firsthand (*top right*). And to get a realistic taste of survival in the bush, Airman Devin McCormick dines on worms, bugs, plants, and tree bark (*bottom right*). It's all designed to maximize the chance of survival and minimize the risk of capture, and it works: Air Force Captain Scott O'Grady credited his SERE training for keeping him alive after he parachuted from his F-16 over the Bosnian mountains in 1995.
Photos by Alex Garcia

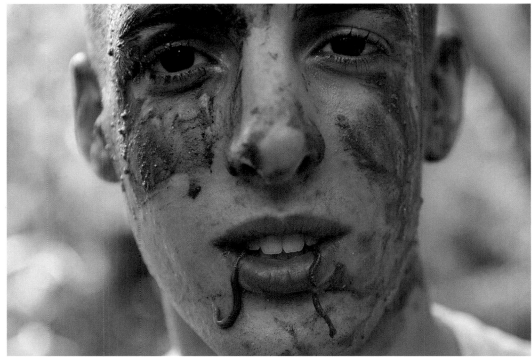

Fort Jackson, South Carolina— "Couch potatoes," is how Staff Sergeant Thomas Gray describes most of the new arrivals at the Army's Fort Jackson. "We call them the Nintendo generation. It takes a lot to get them into shape, but when we're done with them they're in the best shape of their lives, and they'll tell you that." In addition to physical activities like marching and obstacle courses, Army recruits, such as Jason Tedesco (*below*) of Virginia Beach, Virginia, do three hours of pure physical training per day—an hour in the morning, an hour at night, and ongoing "corrective training" (i.e., "Drop and give me 20!") throughout the day.
Photo by Carol Guzy

● *Top*

Great Lakes Naval Training Center, Illinois—"Sleep while you can—you're going to need it" is the advice given to new recruits on the very long day of check-in at the Great Lakes Naval Training Center, now the Navy's only intake point. Roughly a thousand new sailors a week pass through the eight-week basic-training course.
Photo by Donald R. Winslow

● *Above*

Camp Pendleton, California—Marine Corporal Danna Fitch of Marana, Arizona (at left), Master Sergeant Glen Morris of Seattle, Washington, and Corporal Kelsy Daniels from Cortez, Colorado, work out in the fitness center at the Marines' Camp Pendleton in Oceanside, California.
Photo by Peter Turnley

Lackland Air Force Base, Texas—Teamwork shows in the smallest details, as recruit Christopher Klarner helps Benjamin Ecklund with his tie.
Photo by Technical Sergeant Justin D. Pyle

● *Above*

Cape May, New Jersey—
Knowing the ropes still counts
in the Coast Guard. At basic
training in Cape May, recruits
Ruben Trevino, Humberto
Valdez, and Brian Philley
practice tying bowline knots.
Photo by Al Diaz

● *Previous pages*

Annapolis, Maryland—
Dashing to class is standard
procedure for the United
States Naval Academy's 4,000
harried midshipmen—a term
used for male and female
students alike. Inside the
Annapolis dorms, first-year
"plebes" are required to
run—"chop," in Naval
Academy vernacular—and to
look straight ahead ("keep
their eyes in the boat") when
greeting upperclassmen.
Outside, they are allowed to
walk, but must use only
pathways that don't curve,
no matter how much longer
that route may be.
Photo by Sarah Leen

● *Above*

Colorado Springs, Colorado—
First-year cadets stand at
attention during noon meal
formation at the Air Force
Academy. Cadet 4th Class
Jessie Salazar, a Denver
native, and fellow cadets are
studying the contents of the
2002–2003 edition of
Contrails, a compendium of
Air Force history and general
military knowledge that is
required Academy reading.
Photo by David Butow

Annapolis, Maryland—In the Naval Academy's Mahan Hall, a midshipman studies under the watchful portrait of former Chairman of the Joint Chiefs of Staff Admiral William J. Crowe, Jr., USNA class of '46. Annapolis midshipmen develop proficiency in everything from navigation, tactics, engineering, and naval weaponry to leadership, military law, and ethics. Extracurricular activities include drama, scuba diving, and even parachuting.
Photo by Sarah Leen

Cadet Sergeant Lori D. Williams, 21, from Fort Polk, Louisiana

Cadet Corporal Edward Thomas Russell III, 19, from San Angelo, Texas

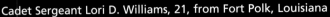

The U.S. Military Academy, better known as West Point, was founded in 1802 on the banks of the Hudson River, 50 miles north of New York City. A four-pronged education awaits 1,200 new cadets, including about 180 women, each year, including a regimen of academics, physical training and sports, military skills, and leadership. On October 22, 2002, photographer John Ficara set up a temporary studio at West Point—including a film-processing lab with a drying rack for the large-format film—to capture portraits of the students and staff.

Colonel Robert L. Gordon III, Academy Professor and Director of American Politics

Major J. Scott Billie, instructor, Department of Mathematical Sciences

🔵 Above

West Point, New York—
"West Point is teaching me, above all, to lead from the front—in an academic or combat environment," says Cadet Matthew Knox (at right), a civil engineering major in his junior year. The school's list of illustrious alumni—which includes generals named Grant, Lee, MacArthur, Eisenhower, and Schwarzkopf—provides the cadets with many role models of strong leadership.
Photo by John Ficara

🔵 Right

Colorado Springs, Colorado—
Cadets Charles Andrade, Jr. (at center) and George Mendenhall are part of the Air Force Academy color guard, which leads the corps of cadets to lunch following noon formation. "This is the one time during the day when everyone is together," says photographer David Butow. "Most of the time, the academy feels like a regular college, with students who are all highly motivated and very smart. When they form up at noon, it's a reminder that this is a military academy."
Photo by David Butow

● *Above*

Fort Rucker, Alabama—Life in the military isn't only about being the biggest, the toughest, the strongest, and the fastest. It's also about common values, positive motivation, and the highest possible standards. At Fort Rucker, warrant officer candidates running through physical training are reminded that the path to distinction starts here.
Photo by Chang W. Lee

● *Right*

Fort Leonard Wood, Missouri—Private 1st Class Daniel R. Reynolds pauses at a rock marking one of the Army's core values. Army soldiers completing basic training at Fort Leonard Wood—which includes 17 hours of values training—commemorate their official rite of passage at this semi-circle of seven rocks. The others represent loyalty, duty, respect, selfless service, integrity, and personal courage.
Photo by Leif Skoogfors

HONOR

● Above

McMurdo Station, Antarctica—
On October 22, 2002—early
spring in Antarctica—the air
temperature at McMurdo
Station hovered at a balmy
minus 18 degrees. The base of
operations for the National
Science Foundation's Antarctic
Program, McMurdo is the hub
for all scientists doing
fieldwork near the South Pole.
The Air National Guard
provides logistical support to
the program, flying in
scientists and equipment on
ski-equipped LC-130 Hercules
aircraft. Here, Air National
Guard members Senior Master
Sergeant Rodney Begin,
Master Sergeant Lyn Garrett,
and Master Sergeant Bob
Smith await the shuttle to
nearby Williams Air Field.
Photo by Melanie Conner

● Right

Kabul, Afghanistan—The
bones of wars past surround
Kabul Military Training
Center, where U.S. soldiers
are training new Afghan
government troops. Major
Paul M. Landry, 39, of the
Massachusetts Army National
Guard's 126th Military History
Detachment, inspects acres of
abandoned aircraft, vehicles,
boats, and armor, including
French World War I–vintage
Renault tanks, Russian
helicopters, and 19th-century
fortress cannons. Says Landry,
"The thought that ran

through my mind was, 'What
occurred to send this piece of
equipment here? How many
lives were lost along with
the destroyed equipment?'"
Landry's mission is to record
the details of the operation
in Afghanistan—from
raw facts to first-person
interviews—for future
military historians, as well as
"to collect lessons for future
commanders and soldiers."
***Photo by Captain Chuck
Mussi***

● Top

Soto Cano Air Base, Honduras—"Being in Honduras for six months is a blast," says Army Corporal Kendrick Dawkins of Spartanburg, South Carolina, of being stationed at the Army's Soto Cano base as part of Joint Task Force Bravo. Although the "hooches" lack niceties like indoor plumbing, Dawkins says: "I'm lucky to get the training I get here. I've absorbed a little Honduran culture and even brushed up on my Spanish."
Photo by Lynsey Addario

● Above

Guantanamo Bay, Cuba—It could be Anytown, U.S.A., minus crime, pollution, traffic, and most of the other irritations of modern life. Behind the barbed wire and guard towers that separate Guantanamo Bay Naval Base from Castro's Cuba, most of "Gitmo's" 45 square miles are much like any American small town, complete with Boy and Girl Scout troops and a golf course with grass greens, but fairways made of sand.
Photo by Larry C. Price

● Below

Bishkek, Kyrgyzstan—"It's surprisingly homey," says photographer Lori Grinker about the barracks at the Ganci Air Base, near the Kyrgyzstan capital city of Bishkek. Base residents add their own home improvements—including decks and storage sheds—to the standard-issue tents. Formerly known as Manas, the base was renamed in honor of New York City fire chief Peter Ganci, who died at the World Trade Center on September 11, 2001.
Photo by Lori Grinker

● Following pages

Attu, Alaska—"It's not the end of the world, but you can see it from here" is what those at the Attu Coast Guard Station like to say about their post at the far western end of Alaska's Aleutian Islands. The 20 active-duty personnel operate one of the few remaining LORAN (Long Range Aid to Navigation) stations. They are posted to Attu for a year—and then receive a month of vacation, plus their first choice of next assignment. Photographer Jesse Diamond spent two weeks on his trip to Attu—the time between supply-plane visits, the only regular link to the island.
Photo by Jesse Diamond

● *Below*

Baumholder, Germany—It's just like home at the Army base commissary in Baumholder, where the groceries are a far cry from what's available in local European markets. Open every day except for Thanksgiving, Christmas, and New Year's Day, the commissary offers more than 10,000 different items to its 33,636 yearly customers. Monthly sales average approximately $820,000—or just short of $10 million a year.
Photo by Guy Tillim

● **Top**

Ramstein Air Base, Germany—It's playtime for Amanda Lloyd and Caroline Sutton, both 7 years old, in front of their school at the base. In an effort to emphasize the importance of family, base personnel are encouraged to meet their children for lunch at the base's elementary, middle, and high schools. "Our children have seen places that most American children only read about," says Stephanie Lloyd, Amanda's mother and scout leader, as well as a substitute teacher at the school. With their two children, she and her husband, an Army major, are on their second consecutive tour in Germany.
Photo by Douglas Kirkland

● **Above**

Parris Island, South Carolina—The shopping is as basic as the training in the Marine Recruit PX.
Photo by Lauren Greenfield

● *Above*

Great Lakes Naval Training Center, Illinois—After the all-night Battle Stations exercise—the final test of his basic training—recruit William Heitman of Redding, California, takes a moment to give thanks before digging into a special graduation meal.
Photo by Donald R. Winslow

● *Above*

Fort Lee, Virginia—Sautéed
salmon on a shingle? At the
Army's Advanced Culinary
Training Course, at Fort
Lee, students learn how to
prepare cuisine that's a cut
above standard chow line
fare. "Basically what we do
here is take military cooks
and turn them into chefs,"
says chief instructor Staff
Sergeant René Marquis.
***Photo by Chief Journalist
Robert Benson***

● *Following pages*

West Point, New York—
The average meal at West
Point takes 20 minutes—with
4,000 cadets at one sitting.
"Plebes"—freshmen—are
required to memorize each
day's menu, as well as the
headlines from *The New York
Times*, which is delivered to
their doors daily.
Photo by John Ficara

● *Above*

Camp Virginia, Kuwait—It's barbecue time in the desert of northern Kuwait, where troops from the 3rd Brigade of the Army's 3rd Infantry Division are deployed as part of Operation Desert Spring. Hot meals with a taste of home have been introduced to build morale among the soldiers, whose mission is to provide an ongoing forward U.S. presence and force protection in northern Kuwait.

Photo by Ron Haviv

● *Right*

Colorado Springs, Colorado—Please sir, can I have some more? Cadet 4th Class Nicholaus R. Koval and Cadet 4th Class Joseph M. Klosinski are quizzed by an upperclassman during lunchtime rituals at the Air Force Academy. Before they can begin eating, new cadets must satisfactorily answer questions on daily menus, current events, and military procedures—and then must remain in a position of attention throughout the meal.

Photo by David Butow

Divers have their feet tied together and their hands bound behind their backs, then must swim 50 meters underwater on a single breath of air. Others are thrown into the pool blindfolded, spun upside down and around, their oxygen masks ripped away, their disorientation complete. It's arduous training, even for the elite members of the Army, Air Force and Navy Special Forces who are enrolled at the Army's Special Forces Underwater Operations

School in Key West, Florida. Along with rigorous underwater training (*below and following pages*), there are poolside "remediation" exercises (*left*) for missing a goal or time deadline. "By the time they are finished," says the school's commanding officer, Major David Hsu, "they will have swum 30 miles and run a marathon." Underwater combat leaves little margin for error. According to Hsu, all training is aimed at making students more comfortable in a hostile environment. The course is challenging due to the unnatural relationship between water and humans." However, he is not surprised that a remarkable 70 percent of all students who enter the program graduate. After all, Hsu says, "They are the best of the best." ***Photos by David Doubilet***

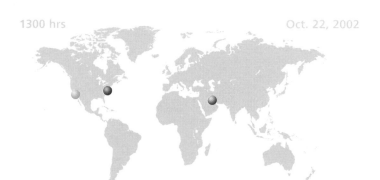

● *Previous pages 96–97*

Quantico, Virginia—
Slithering through the mud,
would-be officers struggle
to keep their rifles dry at
the Marine Corps' Officer
Candidates School. Swamps,
mines, booby traps, walls,
rocks, and barbed wire make
up the obstacle course,
part of a 10-week program

that "tests a candidate's
grit and determination and
physical stamina in a
combat situation," says
Quantico spokesman
Captain Jeffrey Landis.
Photo by Andre Lambertson

● *Previous pages 98–99*

Camp Virginia, Kuwait—
A long way from their base
in Fort Stewart, Georgia,
members of the 3rd
Brigade of the Army's 3rd
Infantry Division train in
northern Kuwait.
Photo by Ron Haviv

● *Above and right*

Miramar, California—In full
flight gear, Master Gunnery
Sergeant George Evans
(*right*) braves the simulated
waves and wind at the
Aviation Water Survival
School in Miramar. In another
exercise (*above*), Marines
must transfer from a wave-
tossed raft to an overhead
rescue helicopter while fire
hoses mimic rain and rotor

wash and a sound system
blares thunder and chopper
noise. Marine air crews must
undergo swim requalification
every four years or turn in
their wings and be removed
from flight status.
*Photos by Chief
Petty Officer Spike Call*

Moody Air Force Base, Georgia— Air Force 2nd Lieutenant Thomas A. Conley, 24, of Exton, Pennsylvania, gets a ceremonial dunking by his classmates after completing his first solo flight in a T-6A training aircraft at Moody Air Force Base. "I tried to escape capture and elude them by running behind a couple of hangars," said Conley, "but all my flight gear slowed me down."
Photo by Staff Sergeant Jeffrey Allen

● *Top and above*

Edwards Air Force Base, California—Showing he's still got the "right stuff," legendary Air Force test pilot Chuck Yeager (*top*), 79, takes the controls of an F-15 in the test run for an upcoming air show. Yeager, who has flown 330 different aircraft, said the show would be his last flight for the military and the last time he would break the sound barrier. One of his successors, Major James "Mash" Dutton (*above*), 34, from Eugene, Oregon, prepares to fly an F-22, the most advanced fighter in the U.S. arsenal.
Photos by Paul Chesley

The Art of Concealment

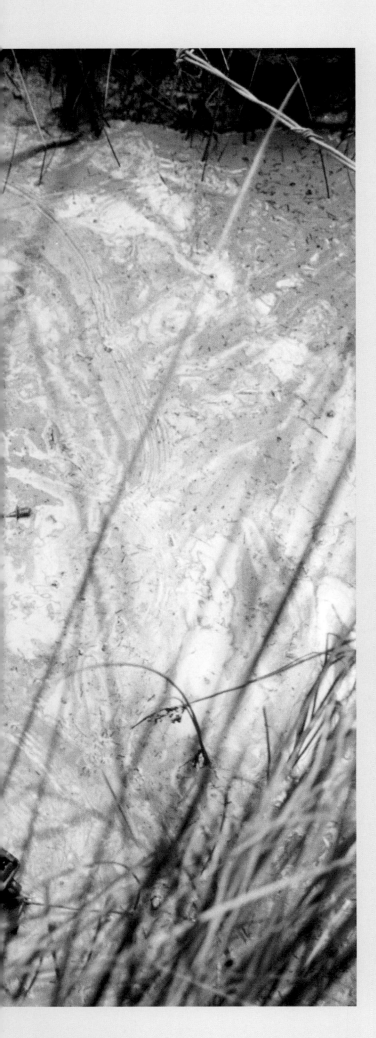

From U.S. Army field manual FM 20-3: Camouflage, Concealment, and Decoys.

Each soldier is responsible for camouflaging and concealing himself and his equipment. Practicing good CCD techniques lessens a soldier's probability of becoming a target.

Exposed skin reflects light and may draw attention. Even very dark skin, because of natural oils, will reflect light. CCD paint sticks cover these oils and help blend skin with the background. Soldiers applying CCD paint should work in pairs and help each other. Self-application may leave gaps, such as behind ears. Use the following technique:

Photo by P. F. Bentley

- Paint high, shiny areas (forehead, cheekbones, nose, ears, chin) with a dark color.
- Paint low, shadow areas with a light color.
- Paint exposed skin (back of neck, arms, hands) with an irregular pattern.

Camouflage a position as it is being built. To avoid disclosing a fighting position, never—
- Leave shiny or light-colored objects exposed.

Photo by Andre Lambertson

- Remove shirts while in the open.
- Use fires.
- Leave tracks or other signs of movement.
- Look up when aircraft fly overhead. (One of the most obvious features on aerial photographs is the upturned faces of soldiers.)

Successful CCD discipline depends largely on the actions of individual soldiers. Some of these actions may not be easy on a soldier, but his failure to observe CCD discipline could defeat an entire unit's CCD efforts and possibly impact the unit's survivability and mission success.

CAUTION: Ensure that local environmental considerations are addressed before cutting live vegetation or foliage in training areas.

Top: *A student at the Army Sniper School in Fort Benning, Georgia.* Left and above: *Marine officer candidates learn camouflage techniques in Quantico, Virginia.*
Following page: *After covering themselves with local foliage, a Marine sniper team is ready for maneuvers at Camp Fuji, Japan. Photo by Robert Nickelsberg*

● *Top*

Parris Island, South Carolina— About 2,000 female recruits pass through Marine boot camp every year at Parris Island. Although women aren't allowed to serve in front-line infantry, they are deployed during overseas combat as pilots, and in supporting roles (including as military police).
Photo by Lauren Greenfield

● *Above*

Camp Lejeune, North Carolina—Members of the 2nd Radio Battalion, II Marine Expeditionary Force on a training maneuver at an auxiliary airstrip near Camp Lejeune.
Photo by Nancy Andrews

● *Right*

Camp Fuji, Japan—Taking a breather before the live-fire portion of day-long maneuvers, Lance Corporal Brian McCallister of 6th Regiment, 1st Marine Battalion, waits for orders in the forest at Camp Fuji.
Photo by Robert Nickelsberg

● *Left and above*

Fairbanks, Alaska—At the Army's Northern Warfare Training Center, soldiers learn to build thermal shelters from snow and sticks—then they bed down for the night in temperatures that can drop to 65 degrees below zero. Dragging their gear on a sled, team members arrive in the clearing and begin collecting branches (*left*). Staff Sergeant Patrick McDonald ties tree limbs together with a parachute cord (*top*); the framework is then covered with parachute silk and piled with snow to create an igloo-like habitat. Sergeant Greg Smith (*above*) clears snow, mud, and leaves from his new bed before settling in for the night. *Photos by Rich Frishman*

● *Left and above*

Camp Pendleton, California—
Marine recruits endure The
Crucible—the 54-hour
culmination of 11 weeks of
basic training. On a limited
ration of food and four hours
of sleep a night, recruits
confront a night-infiltration
course, 40 miles of forced
marches, and a series of
tactical problems known as
warrior stations. Those who
make it through the test are
awarded Marine Corps
insignia and called Marines
for the first time.
Photos by Peter Turnley

● Above

Tyrrhenian Sea, near Naples, Italy—A pair of "yellow shirts," one of them in training, signals the launch of an F/A-18 Hornet from the carrier USS *George Washington*, anchored off the coast of Italy. Propelled by a steam-driven catapult, the jet will accelerate to 150 miles per hour in less than two seconds. When the planes are "recovered"— when they return to the ship—they must hook a steel cable stretched across the flight deck. As pilots touch down, they rev their engines to full power, to get airborne again if they fail to "catch the wire."
Photo by Photographer's Mate Airman Joan Elizabeth Jennings

● Right

Pacific Ocean, near San Diego, California—"It's one of the most dangerous places in the military," says Navy Airman Dustin Russell, part of the flight deck team on the San Diego–based carrier USS *Constellation*. "One false move and you can get blown right down the deck," says Russell, who wears a necklace of "tie-downs"— the chains used to secure aircraft to the deck. Unfazed by the danger, Russell says, "I want to stay where I am. It's kind of like my home away from home."
Photo by C. W. Griffin

● *Above*

Pacific Ocean, near San Diego, California—In asbestos suits with protective face masks at the ready, a "crash crew" stands by on the deck of the San Diego–based USS *Constellation*. The three-person team—one of two crews always on duty—is the ship's first line of defense against crashes, gasoline spills, fires, and other emergencies. Their P-25 fire truck can pump 750 gallons of water and up to 60 gallons of fire-fighting foam. From left, they are Airman John Gonzalez, Airman Jason Richardson, and Aviation Boatswain Mate Handler 3rd Class Scott Pollack.
Photo by C. W. Griffin

● *Above*

Pensacola, Florida—"Controlling the hose is almost as dangerous as the fire itself," says photographer Bob Sacha, who watched Navy airmen practice fire-fighting at the Naval Air Technical Training Center. Mandatory for anyone working on a carrier flight deck, the one-day course includes battling flames on an old plane fitted with gas jets to simulate a crash. *Photo by Bob Sacha*

● Left

Fort Rucker, Alabama—On the flight line, an AH-64A Apache attack helicopter gets a last-minute preflight check. Since 1973, Fort Rucker—"the home of army aviation"—has been the flight school for Army pilots, as well as students from more than 60 foreign countries.
Photo by Chang W. Lee

● Top and above

Fort Bragg, North Carolina—Paratroopers from the 82nd Airborne Division prepare for a jump over Sicily Drop Zone at Fort Bragg. The 82nd was the Army's first airborne division, created in 1942 from the former 82nd Infantry Division. More recently, the division's 2nd Brigade was the first U.S. combat unit to arrive in Saudi Arabia after Iraq's 1990 invasion of Kuwait. "They look the part," says photographer Eddie Adams. "They make you feel as proud as they are."
Photos by Eddie Adams

● Left

Okinawa, Japan—Bouncing in a double-rotor CH-46E Sea Knight helicopter over Okinawa is all in a day's work for Marine Private 1st Class Jermaine Adams, 19, of Shelby, North Carolina. Of the repetitive troop-insertion drills, photographer Torin Boyd says, "We'd land—everybody would get off and secure the area. Then they'd climb back aboard, take off and circle around, and do it again."
Photo by Torin Boyd

● Above

Colorado Springs, Colorado—The view from 17,500 feet doesn't seem to be on Senior Master Sergeant Pat Schraufnagel's mind as he flashes the victory sign at jumpmaster Chief Cadet 2nd Class Aaron Donne. Both men are part of the Wings of Blue, an elite Air Force parachute demonstration team. Photographer David Butow was impressed with their enthusiasm. "There was no hesitation," he says. "They couldn't wait to get up in the air and out of the plane."
Photo by David Butow

● Following pages 122–123

Fort Campbell, Kentucky—It's a long way down rappelling out the door of a hovering helicopter at the Army's Air Assault School. In addition to advanced rappelling skills, the curriculum includes combat assault, equipment rigging, and helicopter sling loading.
Photo by Dick Swanson

● Following pages 124–125

Fort Benning, Georgia—Army paratroopers drop from a C-130 Hercules troop transport plane.
Photo by P. F. Bentley

Beneath the Waves

Photographs by Joe McNally

Imagine a 70-day cruise of the Pacific, at speeds of up to 25 knots and depths down to 800 feet...in a "boat" two football fields long, armed with two dozen of the world's deadliest missiles. Add to that the Navy's best food, 165 of your "closest" friends, and no stops for gas, fresh air, or anything else. That's the life of a Trident submariner.

Photographer Joe McNally went for a day-long training run aboard the USS *Henry M. Jackson,* out of the sprawling base on Puget Sound at Bangor, Washington. Named for its home state's late senator, a staunch supporter of nuclear deterrence, the *Jackson* is a "boomer"—a Trident ballistic missile sub—one of 18 in the U.S. fleet, half of them based at Bangor. Continuously deployed at sea, the boomers' mission is to remain silent, invisible, and safe from a nuclear first strike—and ready, should the order come, to respond, with an arsenal of 24 Trident II missiles and four torpedoes.

"You can feel it," says McNally, of diving to an easy 200 feet. "Everything tilts as you go down on the dive planes and you can feel the pressure changes in your ears." McNally found the quiet efficiency of the sub a stark contrast to the frenetic activity he has experienced on an aircraft carrier. In the "fort"—the control room—highly trained specialists focus intently on their instruments. Even while cruising along the water's surface, lookouts in the open, grate-floored "sail" peer intently through binoculars and communicate through headsets. "The essence of a ballistic missile sub is that it remains quiet," he says. "You don't want to give an enemy any clues about your location."

The main hull is a maze of decks and compartments, connected by ladders and watertight hatches that can be sealed in an instant in response to any

Left and above: *In Puget Sound, a rare sight indeed—a "boomer" submarine on the water's surface—as the USS* Henry M. Jackson *heads out on a training run, preparing for another three-month mission in the Pacific.* Right: *Heading for the dive point, a sailor in the "fort," or control room, watches the surface through a dual periscope.*

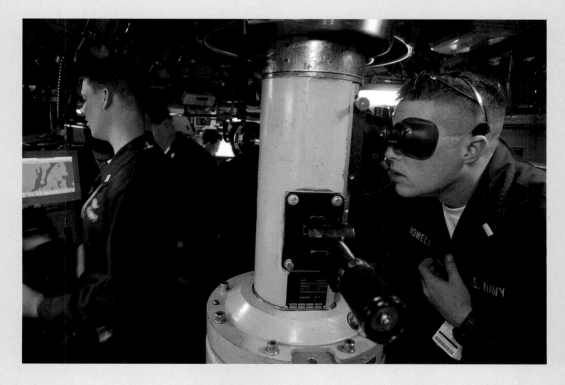

damage. "You can walk around pretty normally," says McNally. "The hallways are relatively spacious—for one person." But personal space is at a minimum. "No question—it's cramped," says McNally. "There are crew quarters in the missile bays. The guys would be reading and five feet from their heads was a missile silo—two rows of them, 12 on a side. These guys are sleeping surrounded by 30-ton missiles, with nuclear warheads ready to fly halfway around the world at a moment's notice," says McNally. "It's an incredible oddity."

But the biggest burden is still the long, sunless patrols. Each boomer maintains alternating Blue and Gold crews, complete right up to their own separate commanding officers, allowing one crew to be at sea while the other trains ashore (not to mention minimizing the time the subs themselves have to spend in port—where they are more vulnerable). As an antidote to the tedium, submariners by tradition enjoy the Navy's best food. The sub is also stocked with plenty of books and videos, and even limited facilities for exercise—Stairmasters fill a number of nooks and crannies around the ship. One problem that hasn't been solved is the difficulty of long-range underwater communications. Boomer men—and subs are one place Navy women still are not assigned—are typically allowed only eight "family-gram" communications per ten-week cruise.

Some of those conditions may be changing. With the end of the Cold War, older Trident subs—the *Jackson* was launched in 1984—are slated to be retrofitted, to become more versatile platforms for fighting 21st century conflicts. Seven conventionally armed cruise missiles could replace each nuclear-tipped Trident II missile. Space could also be made below for a complement of more than

---

Above: Lunch in the Jackson's *mess. Submarine cuisine has the reputation of being the best chow in the armed forces. Right: Checking the launch tube in the forward torpedo room. Each Trident submarine carries a payload of 24 Trident II nuclear missiles and four torpedoes—sometimes referred to as "deadly fish."*

100 Navy SEALs, who will be able to swim out through former missile launch tubes without the sub itself coming to the surface.

But for the moment, you'll find more sea lions than SEALs on the Puget Sound–based submarines. "When the subs are docked," reports McNally, "local sea lions gather on the stern."

Bunking down in "Missile Row," just a few feet from the Trident II missiles (at left). Each of the Jackson's missiles stands 44 feet tall, weighs 130,000 pounds, and can fly more than 4,600 miles.

Back at dockside in Bangor, sea lions bask in the afternoon sun on the submarine's stern.

● Above

Bath, Maine—The guided missile destroyer USS *Chaffee* comes together piece by piece at the Bath Ironworks Yard. "The process takes many years and millions of man-hours to complete," says Navy Commander Tim McCoy. "At the end of the process you take the ship to sea and demonstrate every system before the Navy will accept it and take ownership."

Photo by Anne Day

● Right

Kings Bay, Georgia—A ship-yard worker is dwarfed by the submarine USS *Maryland*, in dry dock at Naval Submarine Base Kings Bay. With repairs almost complete, the 560–foot Trident II nuclear-missile sub is due back in the water within a week.

Photo by Ira Block

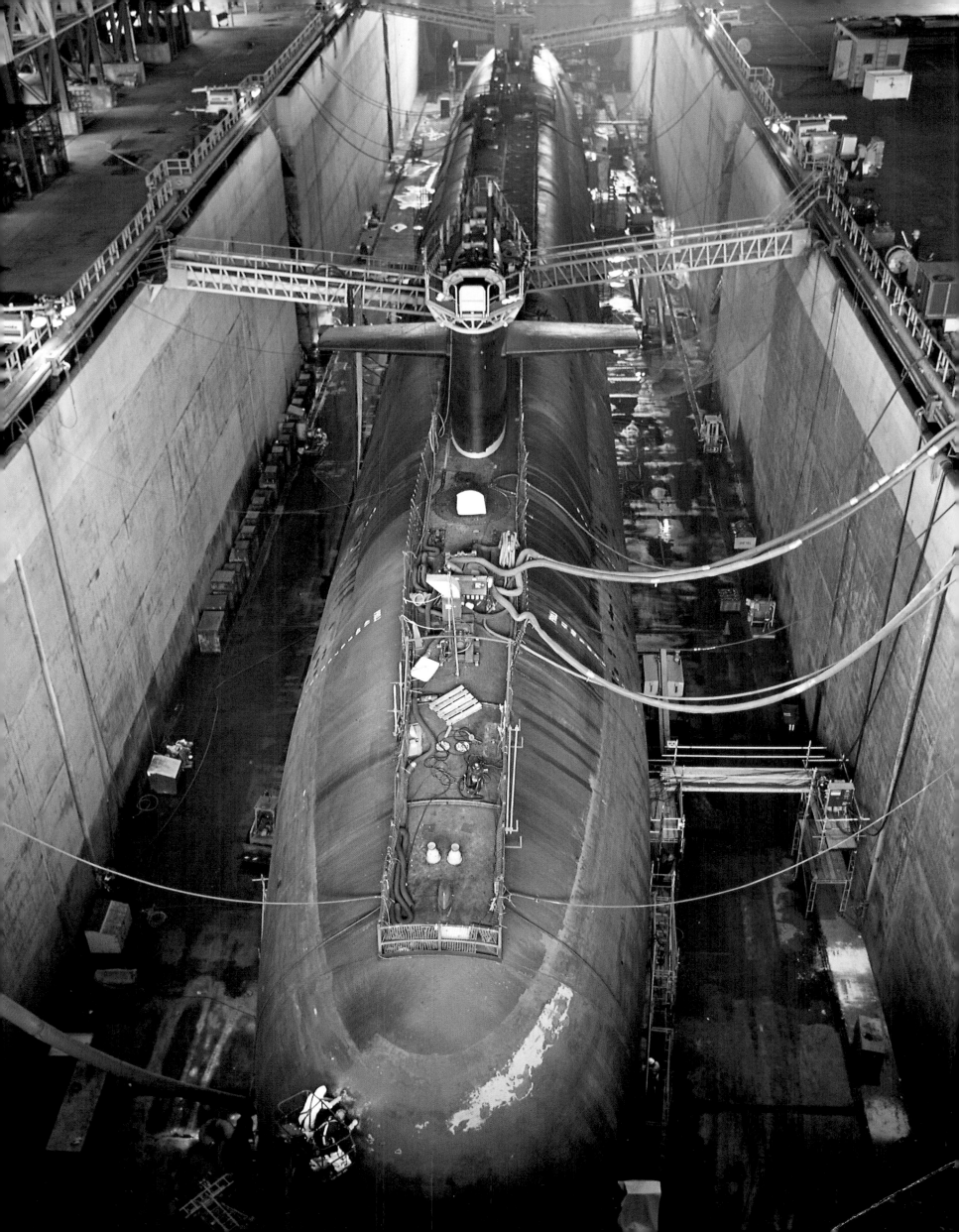

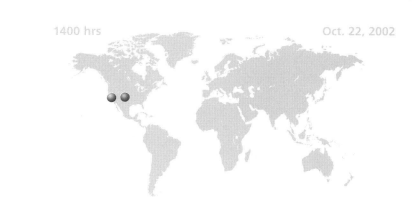

● *Left*

Tinker Air Force Base, Oklahoma—Under the care of civilian mechanic Tom McGrath, a KC-135 Stratotanker, whose main mission is midair refueling, gets an overhaul at a shop on base. All aircraft on the base that are undergoing routine maintenance pass through this shop at the Air Logistics Center.
Photo by Dirck Halstead

● *Above*

Beale Air Force Base, California—Wearing a special jumpsuit to prevent damage, Senior Airman Benjamin Wilson inspects the intake and engine of a U-2 "spy" plane. U-2s have been through several upgrades since they debuted in the 1950s. Flying highly classified photoreconnaisance missions, the planes routinely operate at over 70,000 feet—the edge of outer space.
Photo by Conrad Schmidt

Above and right

Nellis Air Force Base, Nevada— New members of the elite Thunderbirds crew tend to the precision flying team's emblem every day at Nellis Air Force Base. The ritual begins with all four removing their shoes in unison (*top*). They then break into groups of two (*above*), one pair polishing the stanchions that surround the emblem, the other pair buffing the emblem itself with special blue cloths. Finally, all four stand at attention (*right*) after saluting the flag on the hangar wall. *Photos by Ruth Fremson*

● *Above*

Nellis Air Force Base, Nevada—Synchronization is a way of life for the Thunderbird precision flight team. Team crew chiefs (from left) Technical Sergeant Shawn Hardwrick, Staff Sergeant Jamie Leach, and Staff Sergeant Matt Fisher prepare for a flight to San Francisco to perform overhead at Game Three of the 2002 World Series. "It's very different from the 'gray world,' where pilots do most of the preparation themselves," says Staff Sergeant Fisher. "Here, the crew chiefs are responsible for positioning the more than 250 knobs, dials, buttons, and switches. The pilot could go in with his eyes closed and all systems would be ready."
Photo by Ruth Fremson

● *Right*

Fallon Naval Air Station, Nevada—Navy Commander Tom Twomey took this self-portrait in an F-5F over Fallon Naval Air Station, home of the "Top Gun" pilot school. These nimble planes are used as "adversary" aircraft in training, but their lack of advanced electronics means they have limited use in combat by U.S. forces. "It's not a front-line fighter," says Twomey, "but it's a pretty neat plane."
Photo by Commander Thomas R. Twomey

● *Left*

Florida Keys, Florida—A trio of F-15s from the Air National Guard's 159th Fighter Wing, based in New Orleans, Louisiana, roars over the Florida Keys during exercise Cope Snapper 2002. The exercise brought together Air Force and Navy units for joint operations and combat training.
Photo by Staff Sergeant Jeremy T. Lock

● *Top*

Incirlik Air Base, Turkey— "You realize this is real combat, and that people really are shooting at you," says Air Force Captain Christina "Shaq" Szasz. "It brings more focus to your flying." Szasz pilots an F-16CJ jet, enforcing the U.N.–mandated no-fly zone over northern Iraq in support of Operation Northern Watch.
Photo by Ed Kashi

● *Above*

Fallon Naval Air Station, Nevada—Lieutenant Commander Roger "Rock" Pyle of VFC-13—an "adversary" unit better known as the Saints—crosses the tarmac at Fallon Naval Air Station. Although they closely resemble real flags, the symbols on the tails of the F-5 fighters behind him are fictitious. The planes are used to simulate enemy tactics in pilot training exercises.
Photo by Commander Thomas R. Twomey

Top: An F/A-22 Raptor, 22,000 feet over California's Sierra Nevada. *Bottom left:* A B-2 stealth bomber over Whiteman Air Force Base, Missouri. *Bottom right:* An F-117 stealth fighter on the tarmac at Holloman Air Force Base in Alamogordo, New Mexico.

Following pages: A ghostly armada of mothballed planes stretches across the desert at Davis-Monthan Air Force Base outside Tucson, Arizona. Preserved by the dry air, the 4,500 aircraft—everything from F-16s like these to huge B-52s—will be scavenged for parts, recycled as radio-controlled drones, or sold to friendly foreign governments.
Photo by C. J. Walker

Photo by Derk Blanset

Photo by Karen Ballard

Photo by Genaro Molina

● *Left*

Newport, Rhode Island—
Dwarfed by the massive
proportions of the anechoic
chamber, Civil Service
Engineer Pietro Porco tests a
high-powered submarine
antenna at the Naval
Undersea Warfare Center.
The 30-foot-high, 100-foot-
long test chamber was
designed to measure and
calibrate the sensitive
underwater radar and
antenna equipment used by
submarines.
*Photo by Master Sergeant
Lance Cheung*

● *Above*

Misawa, Japan—Wearing
some very serious ear
protection, Senior Airman
Phillip Loper checks a full-
throttled jet engine for leaks
in the soundproofed "hush
house" at Misawa Air Base.
"It's pretty awesome being
that close to a fired-up jet
engine," says Navy Journalist
1st Class Preston Keres. "I was
close enough to touch it."
*Photo by Journalist 1st Class
Preston Keres*

● **Above**

Wright-Patterson Air Force Base, Ohio—LOIS may be a dummy, but she's also the Lightest Occupant In Service at the Air Force Research Lab at Wright-Patterson, near Dayton, Ohio. Among her skills is helping technicians test the effects of rapid deceleration on pilots. One of ten such Air Force facilities, the lab—which also collaborates with race-car engineers on ways to improve high-speed safety—utilizes everything from lasers to a whole-body scanner, which helps improve the fit of flight suits. AFRL scientists are also working to improve battlefield sensors, create stronger, lighter metals, and launch satellites using lasers.
Photo by Erica Berger

● *Above*

Fort Meade, Maryland—
In a "clean room" at the
super-secret National Security
Agency, Army Sergeant Bryan
Witt processes semiconductor
wafers. The NSA makes its
own computer chips as part
of the agency's Information
Assurance programs to
increase the security of U.S.
computer networks. To get this
shot, photographer David
Burnett had to pass through
air showers, put on a "bunny
suit" and wipe his camera with
a special solution to avoid
contaminating the room.
Photo by David Burnett

Fort Gillem, Georgia—Justice Through Science is the motto of the Army's Criminal Investigation Laboratory, founded in Algiers in 1943 to assist American troops during the liberation of Europe. Today, evidence from cases around the globe involving military facilities and personnel arrives at Fort Gillem, which handles an average of 3,000 investigations a year. Civilian forensic chemist David Flohr (*below*) examines a parachute from a case of alleged sabotage in which three Marines discovered—in midair—that their parachute suspension lines had been severed. (Fortunately, their reserve chutes opened properly.) Special Agents James Pangborn Jr. and Greg Nix (*right, top*) dust for fingerprints as part of routine training. Latent-print examiner Clay Allred (*right, bottom*) uses a high-powered laser—and special protective eyewear—to scrutinize an AK-47 for prints.
Photos by Charles Ommanney

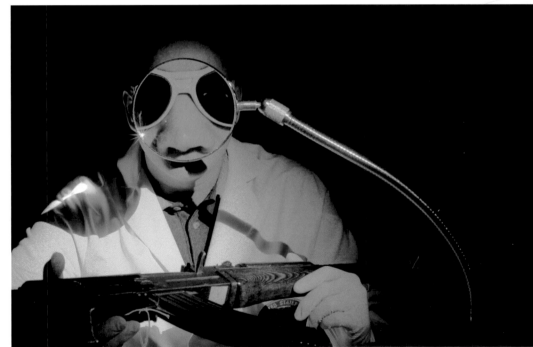

Hidden Warriors

Deep underground, at every hour of the day and night, they sit and watch—monitoring the world on their computer screens, whether below the Great Plains, deep inside a Colorado mountain, or in a war room beneath the Pentagon. Enveloped by security and connected through a worldwide web of communications, they are the nerve system of the U.S. Armed Forces—coordinating troop movements, tracking enemies thousands of miles away, ready to respond in an instant to attacks.

In concrete silos ten stories below Minot Air Force Base in North Dakota (*right*), round-the-clock shifts of two-officer launch crews tend nuclear-tipped Minuteman missiles. Along with their submarine cousins, the 60-foot ICBMs—spread across 45,000 square miles of Colorado, Montana, Nebraska, North Dakota, and Wyoming—remain America's front-line strategic deterrent. More than 300 silos have been deactivated since the formal end of the Cold War. But more than 500 remain active, under the command of the Twentieth Air Force's 91st Space Wing, based at Minot. They are scheduled to be maintained until at least 2020.

Photo by Clarence Williams

Tunneled 2,000 feet into the granite outside Colorado Springs, the Cheyenne Mountain Operations Center (*following pages*) is part of a self-contained five-acre underground hive, complete with medical and dental clinic, chapel, and more than a dozen free-standing buildings. Built to survive all-out nuclear war, it got a new mission in October 2002—hosting the U.S. Northern Command, the Pentagon's lead group for homeland security. Cheyenne Mountain also remains the nation's 24-hour-a-day collection point for real-time information

Photo by Clarence Williams

Right: The farmland near Minot, North Dakota, hides one of the 550 remaining missile silos on active alert today. Above: Air Force officers are stationed in the silo with the codes and keys that could launch a nuclear attack.

about missile, air, and space threats to North America and to U.S. forces deployed around the globe. Its worldwide satellite and radar network follows the more than 8,500 man-made objects currently orbiting the earth—not all of them defunct commercial satellites and other innocent "space junk."

Two stories below the Pentagon, the Army Operations Center—sometimes called the war room—supervises military operations in 200 countries. A communications desk maintains constant contact with senior Pentagon leaders, as well as a database for instantly reaching Army generals. The AOC is also the site of a regular morning briefing for Army leaders and other ranking military and civilian officials—the so-called balcony brief. With the audience seated in a special glass gallery, the briefing officer lays out the current global situation and threat assessment on four giant video displays. Security is always tight: When photographer Barbara Kinney entered the area, because of her red visitor's badge, a warning light flashed and all personnel "sanitized" their computer screens to protect potentially classified information.

Left: *Both U.S. and Canadian troops monitor their borders from the Cheyenne Mountain Command Center, watching for signs of airborne incursion.* Top: *The Pentagon's underground Army Operations Center is the heart of the military's vast global network, operating 24 hours a day, seven days a week.* Above: *Heavy blast doors shield the entrance to Cheyenne Mountain. The center's metal-plated walls have seams designed to bend instead of collapse under impact.*

● *Left*

Andersen Air Force Base, Guam—SEAL stands for Sea-Air-Land—the Navy's anywhere, anytime Special Operations arm. To preserve their capability for surprise, most SEAL deployments and operations remain top secret, along with the identities of the personnel involved. This SEAL—carrying a rifle, knives, bullets, electronics, and swim fins—only agreed to be photographed partly camouflaged by water. Photographer Nick Kelsh reported, "He was movie-star handsome, deadly serious, and had a handshake like a vice grip."
Photo by Nick Kelsh

● Top

Santiago, Chile—Keeping the peace takes practice. Helmeted members of the 82nd Airborne Division demonstrate nonviolent crowd control as part of a nine-nation joint exercise dubbed Cabañas. The "protesters" are Chilean Special Forces and local journalism students.
Photo by Alon Reininger

● Above

Tolemaida Army Base, Colombia—Counter-insurgency training for Colombian Army commandos is the latest assignment for an elite group of U.S. Special Forces and Army Rangers. Here, the Americans demonstrate how to extract troops under fire at a "hot" landing zone. The Black Hawk UH-60 helicopter then flies on to another location, a maneuver known as perimeter control—fly in, secure the area, load up, and take off again. Well-armed guerrillas financed by narcotics sales are active throughout Colombia, and the Americans aren't eager to be photographed. "We don't want the publicity," says one. "We do this because we believe in it. We don't need any other reward."
Photo by Raul Rubiera

Camp Bondsteel, Kosovo— A UH-60 helicopter hovers over the deceptively idyllic countryside on a daily logistics run, bringing food and supplies to U.S. outposts around Camp Bondsteel. More than 7,000 American soldiers are based in Kosovo as part of Task Force Falcon, the U.S. contingent of the international, NATO-led Kosovo Force (KFOR) that is responsible for enforcing peace between clashing ethnic groups. Before the arrival of KFOR peacekeepers in 1999, nearly one million Kosovars had fled for their lives to escape the fighting. *Photo by Master Sergeant Keith E. Reed*

Camp Pendleton, California—
They call it the thousand-yard
stare: Marine recruits test
their mettle during their final
exercises at southern
California's Camp Pendleton.
The three days of obstacle
courses and long marches is
called The Crucible.
Photo by Peter Turnley

● *Above*

Camp Fuji, Japan—On the mist-shrouded flanks of Mount Fuji, Marines conduct a live-fire exercise, advancing in formation across terrain meant to simulate a farmland battlefield, and shooting at silhouette targets. The weapon they use is a SMAW, or Shoulder-Launched Multi-purpose Assault Weapon, a lightweight fiberglass rocket launcher designed for use against tanks and concrete bunkers.

Photo by Robert Nickelsberg

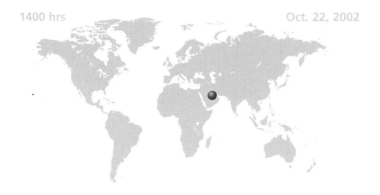

● *Right*

Udari Test Range, Kuwait—
With Kuwaiti camels for
company, an M-88 recovery
vehicle (essentially a tank tow-
truck) from 1st Battalion, 64th
Armor Regiment—known as
the Desert Rogues—supports
tank maneuvers at the live-
fire Udari Test Range near the
Iraqi border. The unit was
deployed to Kuwait in
September 2002 as part of
Operation Desert Spring.
Photo by Ron Haviv

● *Top*

Bagram, Afghanistan—With only his Kevlar vest and helmet—and his extensive training—for protection, Staff Sergeant Mathew Thompson of the 764th Explosive Ordnance Disposal Company retrieves antiaircraft fuses outside Bagram Air Base.
Photos by Captain Chuck Mussi

● *Above*

Bagram, Afghanistan—With a little help from their steel-clad "flailer" and its 72 industrial-strength chains, National Guard members Staff Sergeant Michael Lewis and Specialist 4th Class Jacob "Skip" Phillips clear mines from the perimeter of the Bagram Air Base. Lewis and Phillips have detonated more than 300 antipersonnel and 20 antitank mines. "If my wife knew what I was doing, she'd kill me," Lewis told a reporter. "She thinks I'm doing engineering work."
Photo by Captain Chuck Mussi

Kabul, Afghanistan—On a firing range at the Kabul Military Training Center, a soldier from the 5th Battalion, 19th Special Forces Group based at Fort Carson, Colorado shows an Afghan counterpart how to shoot a light PKM machine gun.

Through the ten-week instruction programs, the American trainers are preparing the new Afghan National Army for company-sized infantry operations. *Photo by Captain Chuck Mussi*

Clockwise from left: Fort Knox drill instructor Staff Sergeant Michael Player; Airman 1st Class Crystal Richardson, part of the Honor Guard at Davis-Monthan Air Force Base in Arizona; a Marine from the 6th Regiment, 1st Marine Battalion at Camp Fuji, Japan; Lance Corporal Jason Bowers, training at Camp Lejeune, North Carolina.

Photo by David Butow

Photo by Brian Lanker

Photo by Photographer's Mate Airman
Konstandinos Goumenidis

Photo by Tom Stoddart

Photo by Conrad Schmidt

Clockwise from top left: Cadet 1st Class Kristin Buchanan at the Air Force
Academy in Colorado Springs; Staff Sergeant Lauren Phillips, a camouflage
instructor at the NCO Academy at Fort Lewis, Washington; Major Thomas
Engle of the Air Force's 99th Reconnaissance Squadron suited up for a high-
altitude U-2 training mission at Beale Air Force Base in California; Army
Captain Shannon Boyle, stationed in Vilseck, Germany; Airman Kevin Carter
aboard the USS *George Washington*.

● *Above*

Nellis Air Force Base, Nevada—Weapons specialists put the finishing touches on MK-82, 500-pound general-purpose bombs. Although the components are created separately in factories, final assembly is done on base for safety and security reasons. Cost per bomb: $596.38.
Photo by Ruth Fremson

● *Right*

Grafenwoehr, Germany—Army Private 1st Class Michael Browley checks the barrel of an M1 Abrams Main Battle Tank, preparing for calibration exercises. The Abrams weighs nearly 70 tons, holds a crew of four, and can reach 45 mph; it can fire its 120mm smooth-bore cannon on the move, day or night, with the help of a laser range finder, a thermal-imaging night sight, and a digital ballistic computer.
Photo by Tom Stoddart

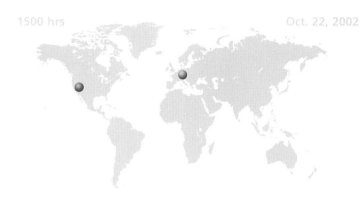

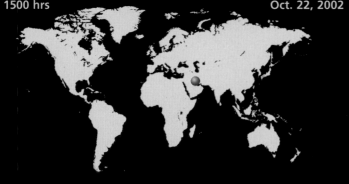

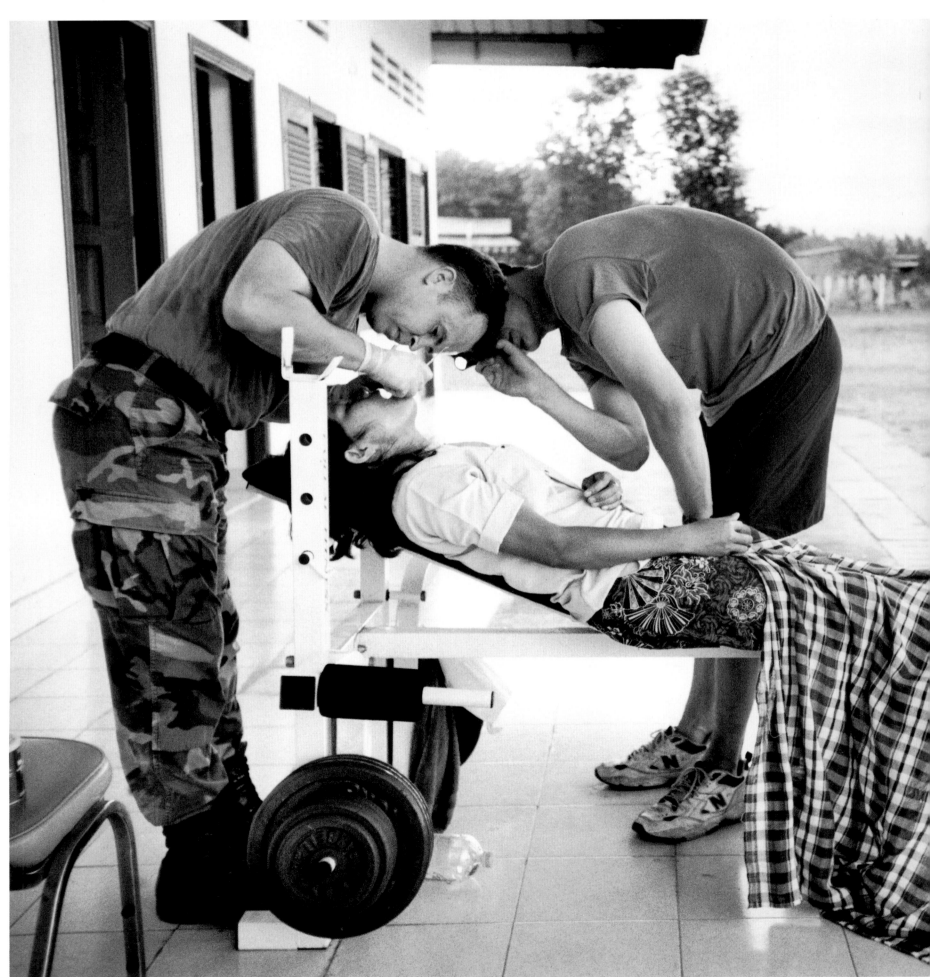

● *Left and above*

Kampong Chhnang, Cambodia— At the Cambodian Mine Action Center, a team of Army Special Forces soldiers teaches medical procedures and safe mine removal techniqes as part of a Humanitarian Mine Action training mission. Thousands of potentially lethal unexploded land mines remain hidden in many rural districts of the war-torn nation, causing horrific injuries to civilians of all ages. In the medical training sessions (*above*), the American soldiers teach Cambodian medics how to insert an IV line, which they practice on each other. Team members also use their medical training to help local Cambodians whenever they can (*left*). Using a weight-lifting bench as a dental chair, Captain Chris O'Brien of Lacey, Washington, and Sergeant Roby P. Lunsford of Tacoma, Washington, remove a woman's impacted tooth. ***Photos by Dilip Mehta***

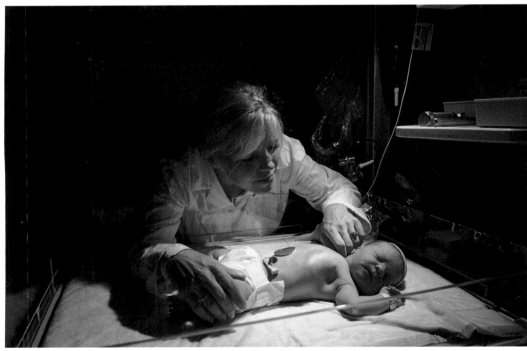

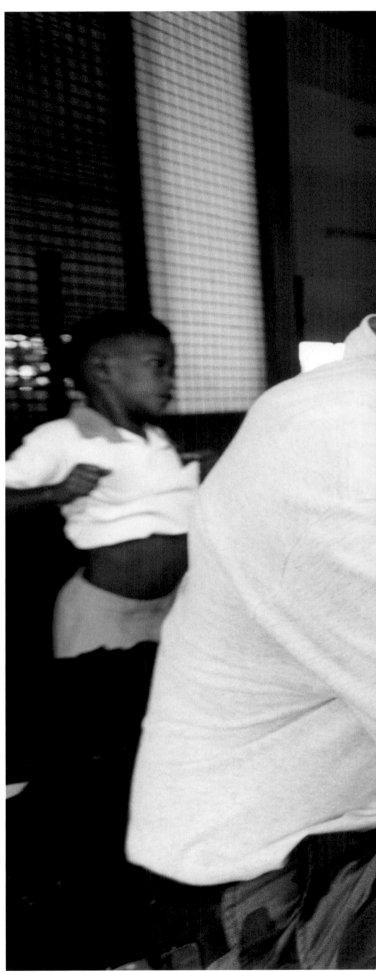

● Top

San Diego, California—"I've always been a strong person, but this was the biggest test I've ever been through," says Lieutenant Commander Susan R. Tussey, a Navy nurse practitioner, of her fight against breast cancer. She was successfully treated by the team of oncologists at San Diego's Balboa Park Naval Medical Center, including Breast Health Center director Captain Melissa Kaime (at right). Says Tussey, who worked with cancer patients before her own diagnosis, "You just have to go with the flow and keep a positive attitude."
Photo by Barbara Ries

● Above

Yokosuka, Japan—Grace Perry, born on October 22, 2002, in the maternity ward at Yokosuka Naval Base. "It's really easy to bring up kids on a military base," says Grace's mother, Jill, married to Lieutenant Vincent Perry, chief engineer on the guided missile cruiser USS *Cowpens*. "There is always a lot of support and a lot of other kids around."
Photo by Catherine Karnow

Palau, Micronesia—Navy Seabees—the name comes from Construction Battalions, their World War II–era designation—do six-month humanitarian tours on the Micronesian island of Palau. Here Corpsman 1st Class Matthew Clark does check-ups on local first graders. Other members of the Gulfport, Mississippi-based team work with local construction crews building roads, water tanks, and other community projects. "It's always difficult to be away from family and friends," says Clark. "I email them every day. But the military is the life I chose, and I find this place very rewarding. I have patients who drive two hours to see me."
Photo by Robin Bowman

● *Above*

Kabul, Afghanistan—"What's your favorite color?" asks Army Reserve Specialist Jessica Peterson, as she hands out crayons to an English-language class made up of local Afghan women, at the Pol-e-Charki School in Kabul. Peterson volunteers in a dirt-floored classroom where the blackboard is merely a painted stone wall. Peterson was called to active duty in June 2002, as she was finishing her junior year at Bridgewater State College. "Since we've been deployed, I've had the chance to teach instead of being taught," says Peterson. "It's quite an opportunity."
Photo by Captain Chuck Mussi

● *Right*

Careva Cuprija, Bosnia-Herzegovina—As a gesture of goodwill, members of the New York Army National Guard, who have been deployed to Camp Butmir in Sarajevo, hand out candy from their UH-60 Black Hawk helicopter to elementary school children in a nearby town. The U.S. continues to maintain a presence in Sarajevo as part of Operation Joint Force, a NATO-led peacekeeping mission.
Photo by Technical Sergeant Andy Dunaway

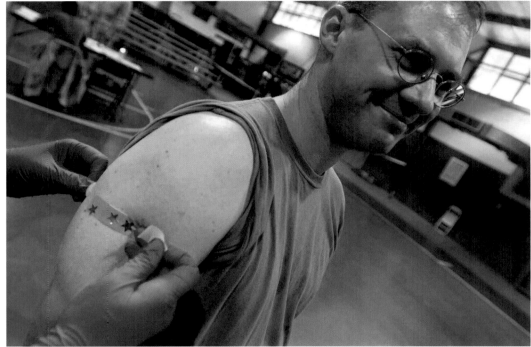

● **Left**

Cairo, Egypt—Combing the streets and hillsides, Lieutenant Commander Daniel E. Szumlas, M.D., studies diseases that could affect U.S. soldiers stationed far from home. A rat trapped in the nearby Mokkatam Hills can help scientists at Szumlas' Cairo-based Naval Medical Research Unit 3 monitor and fight diseases. "Our work doesn't just pay dividends to the military," says the head of NAMRU-3's enteric disease laboratory, Lieutenant Commander Patrick J. Rozmajzl. "Any vaccine we come up with ultimately helps more civilians than military personnel. The fact that what we do has a non-military payoff is a big plus for us."
Photo by Ami Vitale

● **Above**

Camp Doha, Kuwait—Even the Band-Aids are patriotic at Camp Doha, where Army Sergeant Marvin Werve has just been vaccinated against anthrax. The purple gloves belong to Specialist Colleen Raymond, a combat medic and mental-health specialist originally from New Britain, Connecticut, who prepared the special star-spangled bandages the night before. The Army announced its program to vaccinate all its personnel in high-risk locations against anthrax in 1997.
Photo by Staff Sergeant Bill Lisbon

A Soldier's Best Friend

From the days of the ancient Greek and Roman empires right through the First World War, animals were almost as much a part of the military as humans, bravely carrying men and materiel into battle. The U.S. Army still uses horses for ceremonial funeral duty at Arlington National Cemetery, but these days animals are valued more for their brains—and for their ability to do things people can't—than for their brawn. Today, for instance, a San Diego–based naval program trains

Photo by Annie Griffiths Belt

both dolphins and seals for search and rescue operations—saving downed pilots—or to locate underwater mines and mark them with homing devices until they can be neutralized.

Some lucky animals are prized above all as mascots. English bulldog and Private 1st Class Chesty XII was named after World War II and Korean War

veteran General Lewis B. "Chesty" Puller, the most highly decorated Marine. Chesty, who is formally presented during Evening Parade held at the Washington, D.C., Marine Barracks each Friday, is the scion of a long line of doggy mascots, a tradition believed to have its roots in World War I, when German soldiers referred to the Marines as *teufel hunden* or "devil dogs."

For the most part, however, military dogs have to work for a living. Canine personnel, as they're sometimes called, served U.S. allies during World War I—and American forces starting in World War II—as litter bearers, message runners, and in search-and-rescue efforts, helping to drag wounded out of tight, tenuous spots. Doberman pinschers have served in the South Pacific since 1943, when they were the first U.S.–trained military dogs used in combat. A memorial in Guam honors those dogs killed in action (*following page*). Dogs also served extensively in Vietnam, using their highly developed sense of smell to detect both underground enemy tunnels and explosives.

Photo by Master Sergeant Michael C. Burns

Today, nearly 1,500 dogs are on active duty in the U.S. military. Sniffing out

---

Top: *Army Specialist Colin Kingsbury readies horses Surefire and Salty for funeral duty at Arlington National Cemetery.* Above: *Staff Sergeant Jonathan B. Cooper and Rocky, at Luke Air Force Base, Arizona.* Right: *Lance Corporal Matthew D. Morisette of Saint Cloud, Minnesota, drills Private 1st Class Chesty XII, a pedigreed English bulldog, at the Marine Barracks in Washington, D.C.*

25 MARINE WAR DOGS GAVE THEIR LIVES LIBERATING
GUAM IN 1944. THEY SERVED AS SENTRIES, MESSENGERS, SCOUTS.
THEY EXPLORED CAVES, DETECTED MINES AND BOOBY TRAPS.

SEMPER FIDELIS

KURT	YONNIE	KOKO	BUNKIE
SKIPPER	PONCHO	TUBBY	HOBO
NIG	PRINCE	FRITZ	EMMY
MISSY	CAPPY	DUKE	MAX
BLITZ	ARNO	SILVER	BROCKIE
BURSCH	PEPPER	LUDWIG	RICKEY

TAM (BURIED AT SEA OFF ASAN POINT)

GIVEN IN THEIR MEMORY AND ON BEHALF OF THE SURVIVING MEN
OF THE 2nd AND 3rd MARINE WAR DOG PLATOONS, MANY OF WHOM
OWE THEIR LIVES TO THE BRAVERY AND SACRIFICE OF THESE
GALLANT ANIMALS
BY WILLIAM W. PUTNEY DVM C.O. 3rd DOG PLATOON
DEDICATED THIS DAY 21 JULY 1994

Photo by Nick Kelsh

Left: *A pregnant research dolphin named Cascade gets a sonogram from Army veterinarian Major Kenneth Lopez and civilian assistant Taylor Aguayo, at the Space and Naval Warfare Systems Center in San Diego. Dolphins are trained for swimmer defense and rescue, underwater surveillance, and de-mining operations.*

Above: *"Always Faithful"—a memorial in the American War Dog Cemetery in Guam honors the 2nd and 3rd Marine Divisions' K-9 Corps and 25 "devil dogs" that were killed on the island. Nearly 5,000 Marines lost their lives in the battle for Guam.*

above-ground explosives or drugs, along with the requisite police-type guard duty are their primary assignments. At Lackland Air Force Base in San Antonio, Texas, Senior Mess Sergeant James Kohlrenken heads up the Department of Defense's Military Working Dog Training Center, part of the 341st Training Squadron, which was established in 1958 and is the only program of its kind to serve all four branches of the military. Kohlrenken's staff trains 450 human and 300 canine students each year. Using German shepherds and the athletic, copper-colored Belgian Malinois, Lackland's program takes anywhere from five to six months, with each trainer graduating about six dogs per year.

Thanks to advances in veterinary science, it's not unusual to have a dog of 13 years still walking his beat. When a Lackland-trained canine retires, it either returns to school to help train the next generation of handlers or enters the ranks of a 1999 congressionally mandated adoption program. "We find a place where these dogs can live out the rest of their lives in peace," says Kohlrenken, "in front of a fireplace."

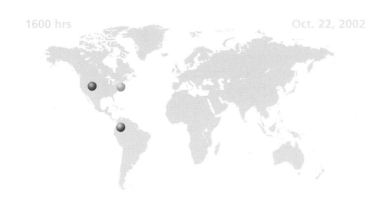

● *Top*

Colorado Springs, Colorado—
Olympian and member of the
Army's World Class Athlete
Program, 2nd Lieutenant Chad
Senior practices for the modern
pentathlon at Penrose Stadium.
The program gives athlete-
soldiers with high national
rankings or measurable world-
class potential—93 men
and women in all in October
2002—the opportunity to
train and compete for a spot
on the U.S. Olympic team.
The program also supports
boxing, judo, shooting,
Tae Kwon Do, and wrestling.
Photo by Rick Rickman

● *Above*

**Tolemaida Army Base,
Colombia—**Army Specialist 1st
Class Jerome Misher works the
speedbag at a Colombian
Armed Forces base, where U.S.
Special Forces are training
counter-insurgency troops.
Photo by Raul Rubiera

Annapolis, Maryland— Midshipman Chastity Lovely and her teammates on the Naval Academy's women's crew team haul a shell to practice on the Severn River. Every midshipman—a unisex term at the Academy—is required to compete in a sport at either the varsity, intramural, or club level. "You learn a lot in sports," says Sports Information Director Scott Strasemeier. "Teamwork, how to win and how to lose, how to overcome adversity—you learn as much on the athletic field as you do anywhere else in the school. It's like a three-legged stool. Sports are one third of the mission at the Naval Academy."
Photo by Sarah Leen

◉ Above

Fort Shafter, Hawaii—"I love it here," says Sergeant 1st Class Mike Fulcher, an anti-terrorism expert at Army Pacific headquarters in Hale'iwa, Hawaii. Fulcher is president of Hawaii Military Surfing Ohana—the Hawaiian word for "family." "We meet after work," says Fulcher, "and we change from our uniforms into surf gear right on the beach."
Photo by Mark Peterson

◉ Right

Misawa, Japan—"The whole point of living in Japan is to soak up the culture," says Navy aviation mechanic Donald Redman, who's doing just that in an *onsen*, traditional Japanese hot springs. Stationed at Misawa, Redman and his wife live off base. "Our Japanese friends laugh at us," he says. "We use chopsticks, they use forks."
***Photo by Journalist
1st Class Preston Keres***

Veterans, active-duty troops, and family members are all welcome at the Hale Koa Hotel in Honolulu. Hale Koa—or House of the Warrior—opened in 1975 as a hotel dedicated to service personnel. Located on the site of the former Fort DeRussy, which was sold as "undesirable" land in 1906, the Hale Koa enables soldiers and their families to enjoy affordable, civilian-caliber R&R, whether honeymooning or taking a well-deserved rest. Serving more than one million visitors each year, the 72-acre hotel complex operates without a single taxpayer dollar.

Photos by Mark Peterson

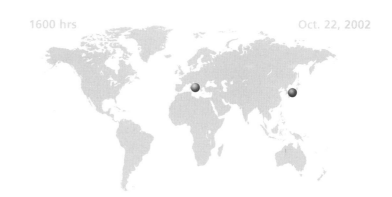

● *Left*

Yokosuka, Japan—The saxophone section of Far East Edition, a 16-piece jazz group that is part of the 7th Fleet Band, stationed at Yokosuka Naval Base. Music is a full-time specialty. "Even when we're under way on a ship," says Musician 2nd Class Jennifer Stewart (second from left), "we usually have a small rehearsal space to set up and practice." The 7th Fleet Band also features Orient Express—a seven-piece rock band—and Shonan Brass, a brass quintet.
Photo by Catherine Karnow

● *Above*

Naples, Italy—In a piazza near the Capodichino Airport, Musician 2nd Class Brian Chaplow of the 6th Fleet Band's Ceremonial Unit plays the tuba as part of the the daily flag ceremony. Naples is home to more than 10,000 U.S. military and civilian personnel.
Photo by Ricki Rosen

● *Left*

Honolulu, Hawaii—Long separations are a fact of life for Navy families. Mess Management Specialist 3rd Class Christopher Brumbaugh of the USS *Crommelin* says goodbye to his wife, Elaina, before his ship sets sail on a six-month deployment. "I woke up the morning after he was deployed wishing the sun would go away," says Elaina, who referred to photographer Bruce Dale as the "tear catcher." "I was not ready to face the first of six months' worth of mornings without my husband."
Photo by Bruce Dale

● *Above*

Camp Virginia, Kuwait—Army troops stationed at Camp Virginia, in the desert outside Kuwait City, are allowed an average of one phone call home each week. Having daily access to email, however, makes friends and family seem much closer.
Photo by Ron Haviv

Fort Bliss, Texas—Charlie the dog waits his turn as Sergeant Jay Polin of Long Beach, New York, swings his 3-year-old son Jacob on the base at Fort Bliss. Home to 12,700 active-duty soldiers, 7,500 dependents, and another 58,000 off-base soldiers, retirees, and their families, the base covers 1.1 million acres—an area larger than Rhode Island. *Photo by Jeffery Salter*

● Top

San Diego, California—
Families are serious business at San Diego's Naval Medical Center, where a baby is born nearly every other hour. On October 22, 2002, Ayden Jacob Shuman weighed in at 8 lbs., 13 oz., courtesy of Susanne Shuman and her husband, Navy Flight Officer Robert J. Shuman.
Photo by Barbara Ries

● Above

Fort Lewis, Washington—
The family that serves together: Army Sergeant Amanda Bechard and her husband, Specialist Daniel Bechard, both of 63 Bravo, Delta Company, 29th Signal Battalion. The couple, who met in the Army, were married in June 2002. "We don't really work together," says Amanda,

"but sometimes when I've got a little free time I'll throw on some coveralls and go help him work on a Humvee." Here they share a few moments at home with Amanda's children from an earlier marriage: Brandon, 8, and Ambre, 6.
Photo by Brian Lanker

● *Above*

Naples, Italy—After three days of liberty in Naples, exhausted sailors wait for an airlift back to their ship, the aircraft carrier USS *George Washington.* Naples hosted more than 36,000 visiting sailors and Marines in 2001, although aircraft carrier visits have dropped dramatically since the September 11 attacks.
Photo by Ricki Rosen

Colorado Springs, Colorado— In preparation for their spring graduation from the Air Force Academy, cadets are photographed in their dress uniforms. Portrait photographer Tracy Murphy (at right) assists cadets with their baldricks—saber holders— and ceremonial sashes. "The cadets are so respectful," says Murphy. "I love being called 'ma'am.' It's drilled into them, that they'd better show respect."
Photo by David Butow

Photo by Lieutenant Commander Scott M. Allen

Photo by Annie Griffiths Belt

Photo by Bob Sacha

The regulations for formal dress in the U.S. military, which can be as specific as the distance between medals or the height of a boot heel, are different for each of the branches. What remains constant is the high standard to which every service man and woman wearing the uniform is held. *Left:* Formal dress inspection is a monthly event for the Marine Corps Security Force Company assigned to the Navy base at Rota, Spain. *Top:* As a show of respect for the deceased, Army guards at Arlington National Cemetery's Tomb of the Unknown Soldier have their traditional dress uniforms impeccably fitted. *Above:* In Pensacola, Florida, Navy officer candidates get ready for final inspection. *Right:* Marines face battalion inspection at Parris Island, South Carolina.

Fort Rucker, Alabama—Newly minted Army warrant officers are congratulated by family and friends at their graduation from the Warrant Officer Candidate School. Chosen from the ranks of enlisted personnel, warrant officers have been a part of the U.S. military since the Revolutionary War. *Photo by Chang W. Lee*

● **Top**

Keflavik, Iceland—On Tuesday, October 22, 2002, a judge pronounced Petty Officer 3rd Class Stephanie Hartwell and Petty Officer 3rd Class Stuart Holloway husband and wife. Both work at the Navy base in Keflavik. "The room was very, very small," says the bride, "so we couldn't invite too many people. We had to be able to close the door."
Photo by James Marshall

● **Above**

Augusta, Maine—Retired Marine Gunnery Sergeant Jim La Chance, 66, enjoys a concert by the Marine Corps Presidential Band at the Augusta Civic Center in Maine. La Chance is Commandant of Detachment 599 of the Marine Corps League. Of his involvement, La Chance said, "After spending my life as a Marine—21 and a half years—I can see that there are things that need to be done and we do it. We do military funerals, we give money to homeless shelters, we attend parades, we even greeted Gulf War soldiers when they came home, at Bangor airport."
Photo by Anne Day

● Above

Pearl Harbor, Hawaii—With her splendidly tattooed husband at her side, Navy Personnel Chief Jacqueline Blaauw reenlists for the seventh time, which will bring her total years of service to 17. Chief Warrant Officer Samuel Rodriguez Jr. (at right) administers the oath aboard the USS *Arizona* Memorial at Pearl Harbor. "The pay and benefits are great," says Blaauw, a native of Elk River, Minnesota. "And the Navy has allowed my husband and me to be stationed together for the five years since our marriage."
Photo by Bruce Dale

● Right

Luxembourg, Luxembourg—General George S. Patton is buried facing his troops in the Luxembourg American Cemetery and Memorial. Most of the 5,000-plus American soldiers interred here died in the Battle of the Bulge, during the final Allied offensive in World War II. Established in 1944 near the headquarters of Patton's celebrated 3rd Army, the cemetery's land is a gift in perpetuity from the people of Luxembourg.
Photo by Paolo Pellegrin

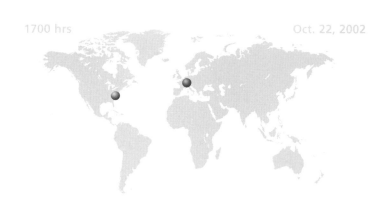

● Left

Grafenwoer, Germany—At day's end the stars and stripes are ritually lowered, folded, and put away at every American military installation around the world. Doing the honors is Specialist Carlos Melvin, an Army combat engineer wearing temporary sergeant stripes as part of a leadership course for NCOs. "A commander can authorize that a flag remain up night and day, provided that the flag is well illuminated and remains in good repair," says Grafenwoer's Captain Scott Gibson. "I was one of the first soldiers in Kosovo—we cut down a tree for a pole so that we could have the flag up by the end of the first day."

Photo by Tom Stoddart

● Above

Arlington, Virginia—The "Old Guard"—the Army's 3rd Infantry Regiment—conducts more than a dozen full-dress military funerals a day at Arlington National Cemetery, across the Potomac from the nation's capital. Most now are for veterans of World War II and the Korean War. The riderless horse (in the third row, carrying backwards-facing boots) represents the fallen warrior and is used in Army and Marine funerals for officers who attained the rank of colonel or higher. Since 1864, more than 200,000 military personnel from all branches, their family members, and some presidents have been buried at Arlington. By the year 2021, the cemetery is expected to be full and will be designated a national shrine.

Photo by Annie Griffiths Belt

Mission to Vietnam: Leave No One Behind

Photographs by Jay Dickman

One fall day in 1972, 90 miles east of Hanoi and almost within sight of the Gulf of Tonkin, a Navy A-6 Intruder carrying its pilot and navigator crashed at full speed into the low, wooded face of Ky Thuong mountain. No one knows if the plane malfunctioned as it headed back to the safety of its carrier, or if it was shot down. The nearest village lay a two-day hike through the jungle. Decades later, a local man who had watched the Intruder go down would guide a team of Americans back to the crash site, in a moving postscript to the Vietnam War.

On October 22, 2002—almost exactly thirty years after the Intruder went down—photographer Jay Dickman took a Russian Mi-17 helicopter up Ky Thuong mountain to meet a 12-person field team from Joint Task Force-Full Accounting and the Central Identification Laboratory, Hawaii. Based in Hawaii, JTFFA and CILHI include members of all branches of the military, as well as civilian physical and forensic anthropologists. Together their mission is to search for, recover, and identify the remains of American personnel unaccounted for in all conflicts since the Second World War. But most of the active cases stem from the Vietnam War era—1,444 in Vietnam itself, and another 447 in neighboring Laos, Cambodia, and the waters off southern China. "Our mission is to keep the sacred promise that no one gets left behind," says Captain Gina Jackson of the JTFFA. "We continue to bring home the missing from the Vietnam War, which helps bring closure to the families and reminds those still serving in the military that they will not be forgotten."

Above: *At the site of a Joint Task Force-Full Accounting team excavation in Vietnam, Ly Thien The (at right), who fought with the Viet Cong in this region, sifts through the soil with JTFFA member Staff Sergeant Kevin McClanahan.* Right: *Red flags on the forest floor mark the places where bits of plane wreckage have been found.*

Dickman's visit came during JTFFA's fifth month-long mission to the mist-shrouded mountainside. Like a civilian air-crash investigation or an archaeology dig, the half-acre site is divided into a grid using string and stakes, with each coordinate numbered and mapped. Loading dirt by hand into buckets, the JTFFA team and a crew of local Vietnamese workers dig down to a depth of 20 centimeters, looking for wreckage (marked with red flags) and "life-support" material—oxygen systems, helmets, uniform material, dog tags—that would indicate the possible presence of human remains. Those are marked with blue flags.

Dickman watched as a 75-yard-long bucket brigade transferred dirt to sifters—shallow mesh screens suspended from a ridge pole, each operated by one American and one Vietnamese worker. Dickman discovered that one of the local men quietly picking through the screens of earth had been a North Vietnamese soldier during the war—and had been the JTFFA investigation team's guide to the location of the wreck.

The largest piece of wreckage found this year was a three-foot knot of landing gear. But enough life-support material also was found to conclude that both the Intruder's crewmen had died here. Next year's visit could be the last to the Ky Thuong site—a final effort to find actual human remains. All told during 2002, 17 sets of remains believed to be from American servicemen were repatriated to the United States from Southeast Asia: nine from Vietnam, seven from Laos, and one from Cambodia.

For Dickman, the experience said a lot about the suddenness, the unpredictability, and the finality of war. "I sat there in the fog," he said, "thinking about the surrealness of it—that 30 years before, this event occurred here. There was the same silence I was listening to, and then the scream of this jet overhead, and then an explosion. It came out of nowhere and was swallowed in this jungle."

Left: *Working on the bucket line, women from a nearby village transfer dirt from the forest floor to the sifters.* Above: *Small pieces of wreckage add up to enough evidence for the team to conclude that the Intruder was lost in this area.*

● *Below*

New York, New York— The Coast Guard's Group Air Station Atlantic City patrols the East Coast from Norfolk, Virginia, to Groton, Connecticut. "I still get a thrill out of flying," says Lieutenant Commander Joe Kelly. "It's like being a kid, standing at the airport, watching planes take off. That I can fly—that it's my job—is just fun. And when you know that you've had a hand in saving people's lives, that's just a great feeling."
Photo by Matthew Naythons

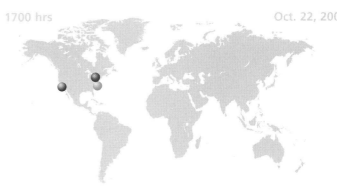

● **Top**

San Francisco, California—
The U.S. Coast Guard patrols
McCovey Cove during Game
Three of the 2002 World
Series. Although no specific
threats had been reported,
security was tight. Fortunately,
the worst news of the evening
was the hometown Giants
losing to the Anaheim
Angels, 10–4.
Photo by Victor Fisher

● **Above**

Washington, D.C.—On
September 11, 2001, the
Potomac river became a front
line in the war on terrorism.
Boatswain Mate 3rd Class
Tommy Roland of Silver
Spring, Maryland, was called
back to active duty to help
the Coast Guard maintain an
active presence on the waters
around Washington, D.C.
The Coast Guard's new
safety-orange patrol boats,
operating out of Annapolis,
Maryland, are more
maneuverable, faster, and
easier to maintain than
previous models.
Photo by David Alan Harvey

211

Day for Night: On Patrol in Afghanistan

Photographs by Sergeant Reeba Critser

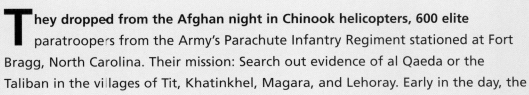

They dropped from the Afghan night in Chinook helicopters, 600 elite paratroopers from the Army's Parachute Infantry Regiment stationed at Fort Bragg, North Carolina. Their mission: Search out evidence of al Qaeda or the Taliban in the villages of Tit, Khatinkhel, Magara, and Lehoray. Early in the day, the paratroopers cordoned off and searched the area as part of a mission called Operation Alamo Sweep, finding only some old ammunition held by some of the locals since the days of the Russian occupation.

But hours after dark they were back, unexpected, and with a huge tactical advantage: night vision goggles attached to their helmets, whose eerie green glow opened up the murk with stunning clarity (*following page*).

One local family was awakened at 2:00 A.M. With an Afghan translator assisting, the paratroopers soon found what they had come for—a cache of small arms and some Taliban material in a footlocker. "Night vision is imperative for missions like this," says Army photojournalist Sergeant Reeba Critser, who accompanied Alamo Sweep. "We can see the enemy, they can't see us—it's that simple."

Lightweight and built to combat specifications, night vision goggles are deceptively simple. Starting with a minimal amount of light from any source—the moon, the stars, a far-off city—the devices amplify and intensify an image, then project it onto a miniature TV screen. First introduced in the 1950s, night vision gear has since seen startling advances. The 215,000 sets now in use by the U.S. military—average cost per unit: $3,500—have been tested to withstand the most extreme conditions of wind, water, and heat. And even more sophisticated models are on the way—lighter still, and specifically designed for urban warfare. It's more than just a boast when the troops who use them say: "We own the night."

Left and top: *Army paratroopers, part of Operation Alamo Sweep, arrive in the town of Tit in Afghanistan and begin patrolling the streets.* Above: *A local man comes forward with a box of ammunition he has had since the Russian occupation of Khatinkhel.*

Above and right: *Using state-of-the-art night vision goggles, soldiers from the Army's 505th Parachute Infantry Regiment search house-to-house in rural Afghanistan for signs of al Qaeda or the Taliban.*

Andrews Air Force Base, Maryland—The commander in chief of the United States Armed Forces, President George W. Bush, heads from Marine One to Air Force One, which will carry him to Philadelphia. Technically, "Air Force One" and "Marine One" are the radio call signs of any aircraft carrying the president. Marine Helicopter Squadron One, based in Quantico, Virginia, provides all helicopter transportation for the president, both at home and abroad. The primary aircraft is a Sikorsky VH-3D Sea King. Air Force One is either of two specially configured Boeing 747-200Bs, each featuring 85 telephones and 238 miles of wire, all shielded to withstand the electromagnetic pulse generated by a thermo-nuclear blast.
Photo by Eric Draper

On October 22, 2002, photographer Nick Kelsh took portraits of personnel based at Guam's Andersen Air Force Base.

Top row: Air Force Lieutenant James Wallace of Charleston, West Virginia; Navy Petty Officer 3rd Class Hoi Leung of New York, New York

Bottom row: Navy Petty Officer 3rd Class Jared Thomas of Las Vegas, Nevada; Air Force Master Sergeant Joe Quitano of Malesso, Guam

Photographer Gregory Heisler set up a portrait studio in a hallway of the Pentagon building, and took nearly 300 portraits of the men and women who work there.

Top row: *Air Force General Richard B. Myers, Chairman of the Joint Chiefs of Staff; Navy Lieutenant Commander Edward C. Ziegler; Air Force Brigadier General Maria I. Cribbs*

Middle row: *Army Brigadier General Mark P. Hertling; Air Force Master Sergeant Alesia Y. Brown; Army National Guard Specialist Sarah E. Serfass*

Bottom row: *Army Master Sergeant Renita D. Crandle; Army Lieutenant General Joseph K. "Keith" Kellogg, Jr.; Navy Lieutenant Andrew G. Liggett*

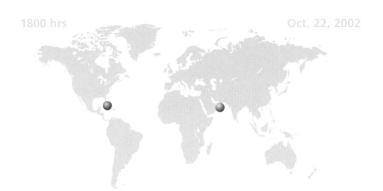

● *Above*

Guantanamo River, Cuba—
Heading up the Guantanamo
River at twilight, Coast Guard
Petty Officer 3rd Class Gary
Przybysz will check the
nearby Cuban border for
security breaches. Ceded to
the United States by treaty in
1903, the Navy's once-sleepy
base at Guantanamo Bay has
been used over the past
decade as a way station for
refugees from Cuba and
nearby Haiti—and, more
recently, to hold Taliban and
al Qaeda fighters captured in
Afghanistan.
Photo by Larry C. Price

Arabian Gulf—Sailors from the guided-missile frigate USS *Reuben James* board a ship in the Arabian Gulf. Such MIOs—maritime interdiction operations— enforce U.N. sanctions against illegal Iraqi shipments of weapons and oil. *Photo by Photographer's Mate 1st Class Aaron Ansarov*

● *Above*

Key West, Florida—During evening exercises at the Special Forces Underwater Operations School, Sergeant 1st Class Robert W. Girsham III of Ladysmith, Virginia, takes aim with an M-4 carbine assault rifle, watching for any onshore "enemy" activity. The kayaks, which can be loaded with up to a thousand pounds of men and materiel, are part of a waterborne infiltration drill.
Photo by David Doubilet

● *Right*

Honolulu, Hawaii—Training for terrorism involving chemical, biological, or radiological weapons, Captain Jeff Korando, Staff Sergeant David Pimentel, and Sergeant Sean Dodge build endurance by hiking to the rim of the Diamond Head Crater wearing full hazmat— hazardous materials—garb. All members of Hawaii's Army National Guard, the three are part of the 93rd Weapons of Mass Destruction Civil Support Team, which

teaches emergency workers throughout the islands to handle anything from water contamination to dirty bombs. "Our unit is hidden in plain view," says Korando. "Every Tuesday and Thursday you can see members of the team climbing the back of the crater. But we're far enough away from the tourists that I doubt many people notice us."
Photo by Mark Peterson

● *Above and right*

Miami, Florida—Much of the work of the Coast Guard's Miami station can be described as old fashioned seamanship—such as checking light bulbs on navigational buoys (*above*). But the base is also home to the Coast Guard's busiest search-and-rescue operation, averaging close to 10,000 cases every year. At right, a high-speed patrol boat heads out from the Coast Guard cutter *Chandeleur*. On any given day, patrols may involve safety inspections, drug or alien migrant interdiction, or marine environment protection.
Photos by Mark Greenberg

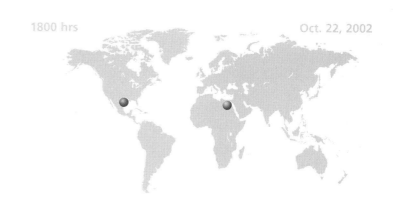

● Left

Houston, Texas—A Coast Guard HH-65A Dolphin helicopter passes the San Jacinto Monument while flying security patrols over the critical refineries in and around Houston.
Photo by Wally Skalij

● Above

Cairo, Egypt—"We'd been here two weeks when my daughter said, 'Daddy, I feel as if I've lived here all my life,'" says Lieutenant Commander Patrick J. Rozmajzl, here reading a bedtime story to Abigail, 4, and Jacob, 6, at their home in an upscale suburb of Cairo. "Living here is natural for them, it's what they do."

With his wife and two other children, Rozmajzl—head of the enteric disease laboratory at Cairo-based Naval Medical Research Unit 3—has been stationed in Egypt for a year and a half, and plans to stay another six months.
Photo by Ami Vitale

● *Left*

Yokosuka, Japan—The sun sets on CV 63, better known as the USS *Kitty Hawk*, in its home port of Yokosuka. A virtual floating city, the *Kitty Hawk* is home to five dentists, three chaplains, two barber shops, and one post office, which processes 1,500 pounds of mail per day.
Photo by Catherine Karnow

● *Top*

Pearl Harbor, Hawaii—At the USS *Utah* Memorial, Signalman 2nd Class Edgar Peavy supervises the lowering of the flag by sailors assigned to nearby Ford Island's Correctional Custody Unit. The CCU, says Lieutenant Commander Jane Campbell, "is designed to get troubled sailors back on the right track, if their supervisors are concerned that they are starting to stray from good order and discipline."
Photo by Bruce Dale

🔴 *Above*

Camp Virginia, Kuwait—
Before turning in at her base
camp in northern Kuwait,
Private 1st Class Kealee
Stewart of the 3rd U.S. Army
Unit plays computer games.
Photo by Ron Haviv

🔴 *Right*

Arabian Gulf—Personal living
space is at a premium on the
USS *Reuben James*, a guided
missile frigate assigned to
maritime interdictions in the
Persian Gulf region. The *James'*
150 enlisted men bunk in
three berthing areas of 60
"racks" each.
***Photo by Photographer's Mate
1st Class Aaron Ansarov***

Hamburg, Iowa—It's about the future for Staff Sergeant Robin Murdock, an Army recruiter holding a meeting for prospective soldiers at a local Pizza Hut. "I want to help as many kids as I can to finance their educations through the Army," says Murdock, who signed up 34 recruits in 2001. Her 14-year-old son Timothy has already decided to enlist. "He says, 'Mom, I'm going to join the Reserves to pay for college, and I'm going to be an officer.'" *Photo by Deanne Fitzmaurice*

Misawa, Japan—"I can't really explain what's in a 'familiar cheese roll,'" Navy Journalist 1st Class Preston Keres says about the food at this restaurant near the Misawa Air Base, where he was stationed for four and a half years. "But they're good, good eats—this place is a real base favorite."
Photo by Journalist 1st Class Preston Keres

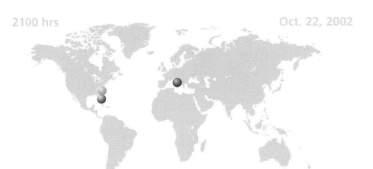

● *Top*

Naples, Italy—In the shadow of Mount Vesuvius, Seaman Larry Jenkins II of Virginia Beach, Virginia, sings karaoke at Capo Landing, a bar frequented by enlisted men and women outside the sprawling Naples Naval Base.
Photo by Ricki Rosen

● *Above*

Pensacola, Florida—It's rock and rotors for Navy helicopter Crew Chief Anthony James Fratto, who cranks up his band, the Imperial Shreds, in his garage in Pensacola. Civilian Chris Haller helps out on guitar.
Photo by Bob Sacha

Fort Stewart, Georgia— Any soldier can audition for the Army's Soldier Show, a musical revue showcasing the talents of active-duty personnel. Those chosen for the six-month special tour of duty can expect a 14-hour-a-day, seven-day-a-week schedule, working as both performers and crew. Here, 1st Lieutenant Angel Stone, Staff Sergeant Gregory McPhee (at left), and Specialist Mark Catarroja charm the troops. *Photo by Anthony Barboza*

● *Below*

Yokosuka, Japan—Out on the town, Damage Controlman 3rd Class James Penney of Ann Arbor, Michigan, and Damage Controlman 2nd Class Steven Bellens of Temple, Texas, enjoy a bite at their favorite yakitori stand. Both are from the 7th Fleet command ship USS *Blue Ridge*, two of 23,000 American Navy personnel, dependents, and civilian workers based in Yokosuka. *Photo by Catherine Karnow*

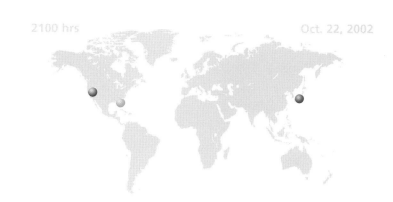

● *Top and above*

Fallon Naval Air Station, Nevada—At the home of the Navy's famous "Top Gun" school, pilots from Carrier Air Wing 8 unwind in the Silver State Club. Usually based on the carrier *Enterprise*, the aviators are attending a three-week refresher course at Fallon.
Photos by David Turnley

● *Following pages*

Pensacola, Florida—Under the glow of a nearby street-light, officer candidates at Pensacola Naval Air Station drill in preparation for their commissioning ceremony. The new ensigns will pass in review for family, friends, and visiting Navy brass. "It was surreal," says photographer Bob Sacha. "It's as if someone forgot to tell them it was the middle of the night."
Photo by Bob Sacha

● Above

Fort Eustis, Virginia—No news is good news for MP Sergeant Marcus Barnes of Greenville, North Carolina, checking the doors of the base automotive shop during his nightly rounds.
Photo by Photographer 1st Class Shane T. McCoy

● Right

Korean DMZ—The Cold War is still a daily reality along Korea's Demilitarized Zone— 151 miles long, 2.5 miles wide and marked by a triple barbed-wire fence. Officially, the elite U.S. infantry troops who patrol it are known as the United Nations Command Security Force-Joint Security Area. Their primary responsibility is preventing North Korean infiltration.
Photo by Michael Yamashita

◯ Above

Misawa, Japan—Navy Petty Officer 2nd Class Donald Rouse and Air Force Airman John Yorde make security rounds by the radomes— short for "radar dome"—at the Misawa Cryptologic Operations Center. Transparent to radio waves, radomes protect antennae and other sensitive equipment from both the elements and prying eyes.
Photo by Journalist 1st Class Preston Keres

◯ Right

Yokosuka, Japan—The guided-missile frigate USS *Vandegrift* sits in dry dock at Yokosuka Naval Base, the Navy's largest and most strategically important overseas base. Most U.S. Navy ships go into dry dock every third year for work on their hulls, sonar systems, screws, rudders—anything that can't be done in the water.
Photo by Catherine Karnow

◯ Following pages 244–245

Ramstein Air Base, Germany—A C-5 Galaxy cargo plane, the Air Force's biggest, undergoes routine maintenance. Together with the adjacent U.S. Army base at Kaiserslautern, the 50-year-old facility is home to the largest concentration of American citizens outside the United States—34,000 military personnel and dependents.
Photo by Douglas Kirkland

◯ Following pages 246–247

Ky Thuong Mountain, Vietnam—Members of the Joint Task Force-Full Accounting team bed down for the night. They spent the day searching for remains of American pilots lost during the Vietnam war.
Photo by Jay Dickman

Photographers' Biographies

Eddie Adams
In the course of his 40-year career, Eddie Adams has served in the U.S. Marines, won the 1969 Pulitzer Prize for his coverage of Vietnam, and photographed seven presidents and 13 wars. He co-founded the Eddie Adams Workshop in 1988.

Lynsey Addario
Lynsey Addario is a freelance photojournalist based in Mexico City, where she works for *The New York Times* and *The Boston Globe*, and frequently contributes to *The New York Times Magazine* and National Geographic's *Adventure* through her agency, Corbis Saba. She was recognized as one of 30 emerging photographers by *Photo District News* magazine in 2002.

Staff Sergeant Jeffrey Allen, U.S. Air Force
The 2002 Department of Defense Worldwide Military Photography Workshop's Top Shooter, Jeffrey Allen has photographed military operations in more than 16 countries, and flown in and photographed more than 25 types of aircraft. His work has appeared in major publications including *The New York Times, USA Today, Time,* and *Newsweek.*

Lieutenant Commander Scott M. Allen, U.S. Navy
Scott Allen has served in the United States Navy as a photojournalist, photo editor, and public affairs officer for more than 22

Cadets at the Coast Guard Academy in New London, Connecticut.

years. He has won many national and military photojournalism awards, including Navy Photojournalist of the Year. He has also worked as a photographer for The Associated Press and washingtonpost.com.

Nancy Andrews
Nancy Andrews was named National Press Photographers Association Newspaper Photographer of the Year in 1998, and White House Photographer of the Year by the White House News

Photographers' Association in 1999 for her work at *The Washington Post.* She has published three books, and is now director of photography at the *Detroit Free Press.*

Photographer's Mate 1st Class Aaron Ansarov, U.S. Navy
Military photojournalist Aaron Ansarov has been in the Navy since 1992 and worked as a photographer at *All Hands* magazine and Fleet Combat Camera Group Pacific. He has won several awards, including third place overall (2001) and a second place (2000) in the Military Photographer of the Year awards.

Charlie Archambault
Charlie Archambault is chief photographer at *U.S. News & World Report,* where he has worked as a freelancer, contractor, or staffer since the mid-1980s. He has photographed the last four U.S. presidents, winning multiple awards in the White House News Photographers' Association contest. He lives in Washington, D.C.

Karen Ballard
Karen Ballard got her start at *The Washington Times,* where she received numerous awards in the annual White House News Photographers' Association competition, the National Press Photographers competition, and from the Associated Press. She now freelances for many organizations, including *Time,*

Newsweek, and the National Geographic Society's book division.

Photographer 1st Class Ted Banks, U.S. Navy
A graduate of the Syracuse University Military Photojournalism program and a Military Photographer of the Year in the feature category (1998), Ted Banks is currently assigned to the Navy's Fleet Combat Camera Group Pacific in San Diego.

U.S. Coast Guard personnel stationed in the Republic of Georgia.

Anthony Barboza
Before becoming a professional civilian photographer, Anthony Barboza spent three years as a Navy photographer. His work has appeared in numerous magazines including *Time, Life, Essence,* and *National Geographic.* Barboza was the associate photography curator for the Brooklyn Museum of Art's 2001 exhibition "Committed to the Image: Contemporary Black Photographers."

Annie Griffiths Belt
Annie Griffiths Belt has worked on dozens of magazine and book projects for the National Geographic Society. Her work has also appeared in *Life, Fortune, Smithsonian, American Photo,* and many other publications. She has contributed to several books including *Baseball in America, The Power to Heal,* and *Women in the Material World.*

Chief Journalist Robert Benson, U.S. Navy
Robert Benson, a Minnesota native and Navy photojournalist, is a two-time Military Photographer of the Year (1998 and 1999) and a two-time Department of Defense Print Journalist of the Year (1995 and 1999). He is the founder of AmericanPhotojournalist.com, and he freelances for *The Virginian-Pilot* and the Associated Press, among others.

P. F. Bentley
P. F. Bentley has covered every presidential campaign and photographed every serious presidential contender since 1980. He is a special correspondent for *Time* magazine, and has won six first place Pictures of the Year awards. His work has been published in many newspapers and magazines, including *The New York Times Magazine* and *The Washington Post.*

Erica Berger
A three-time Pulitzer Prize nominee and former staff photographer for *The Miami*

Herald and *Newsday,* Erica Berger currently freelances for such magazines as *People, Time, Business Week, Washingtonian, Forbes,* and *Life.* Her work has been exhibited in galleries nationwide. She lives in New York.

Susan Biddle
Susan Biddle is a staff photographer at *The Washington Post,* and was a White House photographer from 1988 to 1992. She has won awards in the White House News Photographers' Association contest and the National Press Photographers Association contest, and her work has appeared in the books *Here Be Dragons, A Day in the Life of America,* and others.

Chief Petty Officer Johnny Bivera, U.S. Navy
A photographer for more than 20 years, Johnny Bivera has served both as a Navy Combat Camera photographer, and a White House military videographer. Bivera's images have appeared in major publications worldwide. He currently works at Navy Headquarters at the Pentagon for the Chief of Naval Operations.

Derk Blanset
After stints in fashion, fine art, and news photography, Derk

Blanset moved on to aerospace. He is now a Lockheed Martin flight test photographer assigned to the F/A-22 program at Edwards Air Force Base.

Ira Block
Ira Block has been shooting for *National Geographic* for 25 years, and is a regular contributor to its destination edition, *Traveler,* and its newest publication, *Adventure.* Block was the photographer of *Saving America's Treasures,* shooting more than 45 landmarks, buildings, and sites around the country. He lives in New York City.

Robin Bowman
Robin Bowman's work has appeared in *Fortune, Forbes, Time, Newsweek, Life,* and *Sports Illustrated.* She also spent four years as a contract photographer for *People* magazine, and has contributed to the books *An American Journey; Hiding My Candy: The Autobiography of the Grand Empress of Savannah; Speedweeks: 10 Days at Daytona;* and *Celebrating America's Spirit Together: The 54th Presidential Inauguration,* among others.

Torin Boyd
Since 1986, Torin Boyd has completed a nine-year stint as a contract photographer for *U.S. News & World Report* and has been a photo correspondent for the French photo agency Gamma Presse Images. Boyd is the co-author of *Portraits in Sepia,* a book about 19th-century Japanese photography. He is based in Tokyo.

Dudley M. Brooks
Dudley Brooks has covered major stories worldwide, including the student uprising in Beijing's Tiananmen Square, the first Papal visit to Cuba, and the catastrophic mudslides in Nicaragua. He is the recipient of several awards, including the 2000 Visa d'Or for daily press images, and the 2001 Robert F. Kennedy Award for international photojournalism.

U.S. Air Force members based at the Royal Air Force Base Mildenhall in the United Kingdom.

Christopher A. Brown
A photojournalist for more than 25 years, Christopher Brown shoots for major newspapers and magazines, and has covered Central America, Africa, and Asia. He currently lives in New Delhi, India, where he focuses on cultural, religious, and socioeconomic issues in South Asia. A Saba Press Photos photographer for 10 years, he is currently affiliated with Aurora.

Telfair H. Brown, Sr., Honorary Coast Guard Auxiliarist
Winner of the Coast Guard Alex Haley Award for Public Affairs Excellence and the Military Photographer of the Year, Stand-Alone Photo (1999), Telfair Brown started his photography career as a Coast Guard public affairs specialist in 1980. He is currently assistant branch chief/chief photographer of the Coast Guard's Imagery Branch.

David Burnett
David Burnett's 35-year career began at *Time* and *Life* magazines in 1968. He later joined French photo agency Gamma Presse Images, and in 1975 he co-founded Contact Press Images in New York. His awards include Magazine Photographer of the

An Army MP guards the American base on British-owned Diego Garcia, a strategically located shard of land in the Indian Ocean.

Inside the People's Republic; and *Life* magazine. He has been a contract photographer with *U.S. News & World Report* since 1994 and is a member of the Corbis Saba photo agency.

Chief Petty Officer Spike Call, U.S. Navy
A graduate of the Military Photojournalism Program at Syracuse University, Spike Call has worked in more than 23 countries during the course of his 14-year Naval career. He is currently stationed at the U.S. Naval Air Facility in Atsugi, Japan.

Indian and American Air Force personnel in the joint exercise Operation Cope at Agra Air Station, India.

Year from the Pictures of the Year International competition, and the World Press Photo of the Year.

Master Sergeant Michael C. Burns, U.S. Air Force
During his 14 years in the Security Forces, Michael Burns worked his way into military photography by volunteering to be squadron photographer on several Air Force bases. The winner of more than 100 photo-contest awards, he credits his skill to training by top military photographers.

David Butow
David Butow's pictures have appeared in books and magazines worldwide, including *A Day in the Life of Hollywood; China: 50 Years*

Senior Airman Amanda Cervetti, U.S. Air Force
Basic Still Photographer Amanda Cervetti has been a military photographer for more than three years. She won second place in the Pacific Air Force Squadron for Stand-Alone Photography, and is currently based in Diego Garcia.

Paul Chesley
Paul Chesley has participated in 14 *Day in the Life* projects, and has been a frequent contributor to *Time, Fortune, Life, Newsweek, GEO,* and *Stern.* He has completed more than 35 projects for *National Geographic* since 1975, and his work has appeared in museums in London, Tokyo, and New York.

Master Sergeant Lance S. Cheung, U.S. Air Force
Consistently a top-ranked competitor in the Military Photographer of the Year contest, Lance Cheung's photo assignments have taken him from Bosnia to the Korean Demilitarized Zone, to Northern Greenland and Antarctica. He is currently director of photography for the Air Force News Agency at Lackland Air Force Base in Texas.

Carolyn Cole
Carolyn Cole is a staff photographer for the *Los Angeles Times.* In 1998, Cole helped the newspaper win a Pulitzer Prize for its coverage of the North Hollywood shootout, and was named National Press Photographers Association Newspaper Photographer of the Year in 2001 for her work covering the war in Afghanistan after the September 11 terrorist attacks.

Melanie Conner
Melanie Connor spends the austral summer photographing nature and science assignments for *The Antarctic Sun,* a weekly National Science Foundation publication based in McMurdo Station, Antarctica. Her work has appeared in *The Washington Post, Asia Week, The Oregonian,* and other publications. During northern summers she lives in Hood River, Oregon.

Master Chief Photographer's Mate Terry A. Cosgrove, U.S. Navy
Former personal photographer to the Secretary of the Navy, Terry Cosgrove was recently named Command Master Chief for Fleet Imaging Command Pacific. Cosgrove previously contributed to the *Day in the Life* series as an escort to photographer Steve Ringman aboard the battleship *Missouri* during the shoot of *A Day in the Life of California.*

Michael Coyne
Michael Coyne spent eight years documenting the Iranian revolution. His work has been

published in *National Geographic, Newsweek, Time, Life,* and a number of books, and is held in collections in North America, Europe, Asia, and Australia. He has been a contract photographer with the Black Star agency since 1985.

Sergeant Reeba Critser, U.S. Army
Prior to her career as an Army photojournalist, Reeba Critser was the photo editor at the *Gazette-Enterprise* in Seguin, Texas. She graduated from Southwest Texas State University in 1999 with a bachelor's degree in broadcasting and a minor in photography.

Bruce Dale
For 30 years Bruce Dale worked exclusively for *National Geographic,* on assignments varying from undersea life to the culture of the American mountain people. Now he spends several weeks a year sharing what he has learned, and dividing his photography between corporate, journalistic, and personal work.

Anne Day
Anne Day is a freelance photographer and writer whose work has appeared in *Time, Newsweek, The Washington Post, The New York Times, Fortune,* and *Vogue.* Her photographs have most recently been included in *A Day In the Life of Africa* and *Celebrating America's Spirit Together: The 54th Presidential Inauguration,* the official record of President George W. Bush's inauguration.

Jesse Diamond
Jesse Diamond began his career in photography on his first trip to Africa in 1994. Since then he has traveled the world and worked on editorial projects that range from portraits to concert photography. He lives in Los Angeles.

Al Diaz
Al Diaz's coverage of natural disasters, civil unrest, and major news events has taken him to Europe, Latin America, and the Caribbean. A staff photographer for *The Miami Herald* since 1983, Diaz was part of the team that received the 1993 Pulitzer Prize for its coverage of Hurricane Andrew.

Jay Dickman
Jay Dickman is a Pulitzer Prize–winning photographer and a regular contributor to *National Geographic.* He has worked on nearly all of the *Day in the Life* books, as well as on *Passage to Vietnam.* Dickman's work has also earned him the World Press Photo Golden Eye award.

David Doubilet
A contributing photographer-in-residence at the National Geographic Society, David

Doubilet has produced more than 60 stories for the organization's magazine. He is an honorary fellow of the Royal Photographic Society of Great Britain and the recipient of numerous awards and commendations, including the Lennart Nilsson Award for photography from the Karolinska Institute in Stockholm.

Eric Draper
Eric Draper joined the Associated Press in 1993 and has been awarded the Associated Press Managing Editors award three consecutive times. He won a 1999 National Headliner award and was named Photographer of the Year in 1992 by the Scripps Howard newspaper group. He is currently the White House photo director and personal photographer for President George W. Bush.

Technical Sergeant Andy Dunaway, U.S. Air Force
The 2001 Department of Defense Military Photographer of the Year Winner for Combat Camera, Andy Dunaway is currently serving as the national advertising photographer for the Air Force

The Sea Air Rescue (SAR) unit at Naval Air Station Whidbey Island, Washington.

Recruiting Service. He is also a photojournalist for *Stars and Stripes* Pacific edition in Seoul, Korea. Dunaway is a veteran of operations Desert Storm, Allied Force, and Enduring Freedom.

Lieutenant Colonel Michael Edgerington, U.S. Army
Michael Edrington has been a soldier, combat photographer, and public affairs officer for more than 25 years. He was co-curator of a photo exhibit on Operation Desert Storm at the Smithsonian Institution's National Museum of American History, and he has

Aboard the Coast Guard cutter Sundew *in Duluth, Minnesota.*

photographed for United Press International, *The Washington Post,* and Random House.

Paul Fetters
After studying photojournalism at the University of Missouri, Paul Fetters spent five years in New York City shooting for *USA Today, Time, Newsweek,* and other publications. Today, with more than 20 years of photojournalism experience, Fetters travels the world on assignment for corporate, nonprofit, and editorial clients.

John Ficara
John Ficara has traveled the globe as an editorial photographer, covering the White House for *Newsweek* through four administrations. He has produced 26 cover images for *Newsweek,* as well as covers for a variety of international magazines. His awards include a Desi and a National Headliner. He lives in the Washington, D.C., area

Victor Fisher
Victor Fisher is a photographer, editor, and Internet imaging consultant. Working with the Associated Press in New York City, he covered stories from the Olympics to the Oklahoma City bombing. Fisher works in traditional and digital media, and has been widely published throughout the world.

Deanne Fitzmaurice
Deanne Fitzmaurice has been a staff photographer at the *San Francisco Chronicle* for 14 years. She has won numerous awards from the Society of Professional Journalists and the National Press Photographers Association, and has been published in several books and national magazines including *Time, Newsweek, People,* and *Sports Illustrated.*

Petty Officer 1st Class Sarah Foster-Snell, U.S. Coast Guard
Sarah Foster-Snell's first tour of duty as a Coast Guard photographer was aboard the cutter

Rush, on patrols from homeport Honolulu to Alaska, Russia, and Polynesia. She is a recipient of the Coast Guard Alex Haley Award and the Department of Defense Thomas Jefferson Award for excellence in photojournalism.

Ruth Fremson
Ruth Fremson has worked as a staff photographer at *The Washington Times,* the Associated Press, and *The New York Times.* She has won three Pulitzer prizes: the 1999 prize in feature photography for coverage of President Clinton's impeachment proceedings; the 2002 prize in spot news for coverage of the September 11 attacks; and the 2002 prize in feature photography for coverage of Pakistan and Afghanistan.

Rich Frishman
Specializing in intimate photo essays, illustrative photo mosaics, and environmental portraiture, Rich Frishman produces work for many national and international magazines. A photographic storyteller, Frishman began his career in newspapers, garnering dozens of prestigious national awards over the past 30 years.

Paul Fusco
Paul Fusco began shooting photographs in the U.S. Army Signal Corps in Korea between

American Army Special Forces troops train Georgian soldiers in small arms tactics in Tbilisi, Republic of Georgia.

1951 and 1953. After the war he studied photojournalism and became a staff photographer with *Look* magazine. His photography has been published in *Time, Life, Newsweek, The New York Times Magazine,* and others, and he is the author of several books. Fusco has been a member of Magnum Photos since 1974.

Alex Garcia
A staff photographer for the *Chicago Tribune,* Alex Garcia won a Golden Eye award from World Press Photo in 2002. He shared a Pulitzer Prize in explanatory reporting in 2001 as part of a team that documented gridlock at O'Hare Airport. In 2002, Garcia was named Illinois Press Photographer of the Year.

Liz Gilbert
Liz Gilbert has spent the past ten years working as a photojournalist in Africa, recently shooting for *A Day in the Life of Africa.* Her pictures have appeared in *Time, Newsweek, The New York Times,* and many European publications, and has been exhibited at the Visa pour l'Image festival.

David Gilkey
David Gilkey has photographed the fall of Apartheid in South Africa, famine in Somalia, tribal warfare in Rwanda, and the violent conflict in Kosovo. He is a staff photographer with the *Detroit Free Press* and has been a consistent award-winner in state, national, and international competitions.

Technical Sergeant Efrain Gonzalez, U.S. Air Force
The 1998 Department of Defense Military Photography Workshop Top Shooter, and a graduate of the Rochester Institute of Technology Military Photojournalism program, Efrain Gonzalez has documented combat operations in Iraq, Bosnia, Albania, Macedonia, and Afghanistan. He is a veteran of operations Desert Storm, Allied Force, and Enduring Freedom.

Photographer's Mate Airman Konstandinos S. Goumenidis, U.S. Navy
Konstandinos Goumenidis joined the U.S. Navy two years ago, where he has had the opportunity to pursue his lifelong interest in photography. His pictures have appeared in *Navy Times* and on the Navy Newsstand website.

Arthur Grace
A former U.S. Marine, Arthur Grace has covered stories internationally as a *Newsweek* staff photographer, and as a contract photographer for *Time.* Through his affiliation with the Sygma photo agency, his photos have appeared on the cover of leading publications including *Life, Time, Newsweek, Paris Match, Stern,* and *The New York Times Magazine.*

A Marine stationed in Rabat, Morocco, for embassy guard-duty enjoys some time off.

Mark Greenberg
A former photo assignment editor for the Associated Press, Mark Greenberg co-founded the New York-based agency Visions Photo and is principal and director of development for the start-up photo agency World Picture News. He was nominated for a Pulitzer Prize for feature photography, and has won several World Press Photo awards

Stanley Greene
Stanley Greene has covered such events as the fall of the Berlin Wall, the breakup of the Soviet Union, and the Chechen rebellion for publications including the *San Francisco Examiner, Newsweek, Rolling Stone,* and *Newsday.* He received World Press Photo awards in 1993 and 2001. Based in Paris, he has been a member of the VU photo agency since 1991.

Lauren Greenfield
Lauren Greenfield's work has been exhibited internationally, and appears regularly in *The New York Times Magazine, The New Yorker, National Geographic, Harper's Bazaar,* and *Time.* Her books include *Fast Forward: Growing Up in the Shadow of Hollywood;* and

Girl Culture. She is a member of the VII photo agency and lives in Venice, California.

C. W. Griffin
C. W. Griffin spent seven years as a special missions combat photographer, and was the first black photographer to win Military Photographer of the Year for all branches of the armed forces. In July of 1983 he joined the staff of *The Miami Herald.* His work has appeared on the covers of both *The African Americans* and *Florida Hurricane and Disaster 1992.*

Lori Grinker
Lori Grinker began her photographic career while still a student at New York's Parsons School of Design, documenting the rise of 13-year-old boxer Mike Tyson. In addition to publishing a book, *The Invisible Thread: A Portrait of Jewish American Women,* Grinker has had her work exhibited and published worldwide.

Jack Gruber
Currently a staff photographer for *USA Today,* Jack Gruber has also worked as a staff photographer for *The Flint Journal* (Michigan), *The Detroit News,* and the *Commercial Appeal* in Memphis, Tennessee. Gruber won the William Randolph Hearst Photojournalism Championship in 1989. He lives in San Francisco.

Carol Guzy
Carol Guzy spent eight years at *The Miami Herald* before moving to Washington, D.C. in 1988, where she is a staff photographer at *The Washington Post.* She has been honored twice with the Pulitzer Prize for spot news and received a third Pulitzer for feature photography.

Dirck Halstead
Dirck Halstead is editor and publisher of *The Digital Journalist* (digitaljournalist.org), the monthly online magazine for photojournalism. At 17, he became *Life*

A military mom carries her two daughters home from the base day-care center at the Naval Construction Training Center in Gulfport, Mississippi.

1st Lieutenant Tana Hamilton

magazine's youngest combat photographer while covering the Guatemalan Civil War. In 1972 he accepted a contract with *Time,* and covered the White House for the next 29 years. He lives in Austin, Texas.

First Lieutenant Tana R. Hamilton, U.S. Air Force
Named 1995's Military Sports Photojournalist of the Year, Tana Hamilton is a graduate of the Rochester Institute of Technology Military Photojournalism Program and of Regents College in New York. She is currently a public affairs officer at Wright-Patterson Air Force Base in Ohio.

David Alan Harvey
A former National Press Photographers Association Magazine Photographer of the Year, David Alan Harvey has been a member of Magnum Photos since 1993. He has photographed more than 35 articles for *National Geographic,* on subjects including the Wyeth family, Cuba, Berlin, Vietnam, and Chile. His project on Spain was exhibited at the 1997 International Festival of Photojournalism in Perpignan, France.

Ron Haviv
A contract photographer for *Newsweek,* Ron Haviv's work is published by magazines throughout the world, including *Stern, Paris Match,* and *The New York Times Magazine.* His photographs have earned World Press, Pictures of the Year, and Overseas Press Club of America awards, as well as the Leica Medal of Excellence. He is a founding member of the VII photo agency.

Gregory Heisler
Gregory Heisler is best known for his trademark editorial portrait covers and essays for *Time, Life, Sports Illustrated, GQ,* and *Esquire,* among others. His numerous awards include the Leica Medal of Excellence (1988) and the World Image Award (1991). He lives in New York City.

Gunnery Sergeant Matt Hevezi, U.S. Marine Corps
From serving in Kuwait and Iraq as a public affairs chief with the 1st Marine Expeditionary Force, to covering the Los Angeles riots as a combat photographer, Matt Hevezi's military photojournalism career has taken him around the world. Hevezi is a distinguished graduate of Syracuse University's Military Photojournalism Program.

Photographer's Mate 2nd Class Robert S. Houlihan, U.S. Navy
As a Navy photojournalist, Robert Houlihan has traveled to more than 15 countries to tell the Navy story. Houlihan is a graduate of the Military Photojournalism program at Syracuse University and is currently serving as a photo editor and photojournalist for the Navy's *All Hands* magazine.

Nikolai Ignatiev
Based in Moscow and London, Nikolai Ignatiev took up photography in 1982, and has worked on assignment for *Time, Life, Newsweek, Stern, Der Spiegel, GEO, The Sunday Times* (London), *Vogue,* and other publications. He participated in *A Day in the Life of the Soviet Union* and *24 Hours in Cyberspace,* and is represented by the Network Photographers photo agency.

At Anniston Army Depot in Alabama, a member of the 722nd Explosive Ordnance company (EOD) dons a suit worn to defuse bombs.

Photographer 2nd Class Jennifer Smith

Photographer's Mate Airman Joan Elizabeth Jennings, U.S. Navy
Born near Panama City, Panama, Joan Jennings began her Navy career in March of 2001. Her love of photography began in childhood when her cousin gave her a camera as a Christmas gift. She is currently serving aboard the aircraft carrier USS *George Washington.*

Catherine Karnow
A specialist in photographing people, Catherine Karnow has been published in numerous international magazines including French and German *GEO, National Geographic,* and *Smithsonian.* Her book projects include *Passage to Vietnam, Women in the Material World,* and several books in the *Day in the Life* series. Born and raised in Hong Kong, she now lives in San Francisco.

Ed Kashi
Ed Kashi has worked in nearly 60 countries and has been published extensively all over the world in *National Geographic, The New York Times Magazine, Time, Fortune, Newsweek,* and *Smithsonian,* among others. His work has received numerous prizes, including the World Press Photo and Pictures of the Year awards. He lives in San Francisco.

Staff Sergeant Gary L. Kieffer, U.S. Army
A former staff photographer for *U.S. News & World Report,* Staff Sergeant Gary Kieffer began his photographic career with the U.S. Army in 1973. His photographs have appeared in national publications including *Newsweek, Time,* the *Los Angeles Times,* and *USA Today.* He is currently on active duty in the Army Reserves with the U.S. European Command, Stuttgart, Germany.

David Hume Kennerly
Winner of the 1972 Pulitzer Prize for feature photography, David Hume Kennerly is a photographer

and journalist whose credits include serving as personal photographer to President Gerald R. Ford and as contributing editor for *Newsweek.* His books include *Shooter, Photo Op, Sein Off,* and *Photo du Jour.* He is the executive producer of *A Day in the Life of the United States Armed Forces.*

Journalist 1st Class Preston Keres, U.S. Navy
As the 2000 and 2001 Military Photographer of the Year, Preston Keres has traveled the world documenting the military story,

An F-16 fighter jet stationed at Osan Air Base in South Korea supports reconnaissance aircraft monitoring North Korea.

Photographer 1st Class Ted Banks

including the aftermath of the World Trade Center attack, the 2002 Winter Olympic Games, and operations in the Persian Gulf. He is on the staff of the Navy's award-winning *All Hands* magazine.

Barbara Kinney
Barbara Kinney has worked as an editor and photographer for *USA Today,* as a freelance photographer in Washington, D.C., as the global entertainment picture editor for Reuters news service, and as one of four personal photographers for President Bill Clinton. In 1996, she received a first place in the World Press Photo competition.

Douglas Kirkland
Douglas Kirkland's 40-year career in photography began at *Look* and, later, *Life* magazines during the 1960s' golden age of photojournalism. He has extensively photographed celebrity subjects, including Marilyn Monroe and Robert Redford, and has published six books. His fine-art photography has been exhibited in Asia, Europe, and the United States.

Andre Lambertson
Winner of four Picture of the Year awards and a World Press Photo award, Andre Lambertson is a staff photographer with *Time* magazine. His work has been exhibited at the Smithsonian Institution, and was honored with a special award

by Perpignan's Visa pour l'Image photojournalism festival. He lives in New York.

Brian Lanker
Brian Lanker's long career in photography has won him numerous awards, including the 1973 Pulitzer Prize for feature photography and Newspaper Photographer of the Year in 1970 and 1976. Lanker's book of portraits, *I Dream a World: Portraits of Black Women Who Changed America,* is currently in its 14th printing.

Chang W. Lee
Chang Lee has been a staff photographer at *The New York Times* since 1994, covering the 1998 Nagano Olympics, the 1999 Colombia earthquake, the 2000 presidential primaries and Republican National Convention, five World Series, and three Stanley Cups. He has published several books through *The New York Times* and the Smithsonian Society.

Sarah Leen
Since 1988, Sarah Leen has worked as a photographer for *National Geographic* magazine. Her 15 published assignments include the Kamchatka peninsula in Siberia and the Mexican volcano Popocatepetl. A book of her work, *American Back Roads,* was published in 2000. She lives in Edgewater, Maryland.

Barry Lewis
Barry Lewis began his career in photography in 1976, winning the *Vogue* Award while working as a staff photographer for that magazine. Since then, he has worked as a freelance photographer, publishing and exhibiting his work around the world and winning awards, including the World Press Oscar Barnak Award in 1991. He is a founder of the Network Photographers agency.

251

Staff Sergeant Bill Lisbon, U.S. Marine Corps

Public affairs chief for a nuclear, biological, and chemical response force in Kuwait, Bill Lisbon is a recent graduate of Syracuse University's military photojournalism program. His work appears on the cover of the book *Making the Corps* by Thomas Ricks, and he has won multiple military photojournalism awards.

Staff Sergeant Jeremy T. Lock, U.S. Air Force

Jeremy Lock got his start as an aerial photographer at Vandenberg Air Force Base. He studied photojournalism at Syracuse University, and was assigned to the 1st Orbit Camera Squadron at Charleston Air Force Base, South Carolina, after graduating at the top of his class. In 2001 he took second place in the Military Photographer of the Year contest.

James Marshall

James Marshall has traveled extensively as a photographer for more than 20 years, and holds producer credits on several photographic titles, including *Hong Kong: Here Be Dragons; Planet Vegas;* and *A Day in the Life of Thailand.* His work has been exhibited on several continents and published in most major magazines. Marshall is represented by Corbis and The Image Works.

Photographer 1st Class Shane T. McCoy, U.S. Navy

Combat photographer Shane McCoy has documented military operations and exercises in 28 countries. His photographs have

routinely been used for Joint Chiefs of Staff and Secretary of Defense briefings, and have been published internationally in books, newspapers, and magazines. He is currently at the Navy's *All Hands* magazine.

Joe McNally

Described by *American Photo* magazine as "perhaps the most versatile photojournalist working today," Joe McNally has received numerous awards from Pictures of the Year, World Press Photo, *American Photo,* and the Art Directors Club. "Faces of Ground Zero," his exhibition of portraits made with a giant Polaroid camera in the wake of the September 11 attacks, toured the country after an opening at Grand Central Station, and was published in the book *One Nation.*

Robert McNeely

Robert McNeely became interested in photography while serving in the U.S. Army in Vietnam. Since then, he has worked as a campaign photographer for George McGovern in 1972, as an official White House photographer in 1976, and as the personal photographer to President Bill Clinton.

Dilip Mehta

New Delhi–based Dilip Mehta has published pictorial essays in *Time, National Geographic, Newsweek, The New York Times, GEO, Le Figaro,* and many other magazines and newspapers. He has contributed to nearly every *Day in the Life* book, and is represented by Contact Press Images.

Photographer's Mate 2nd Class Andrew Meyers

A military photographer for seven years, Andrew Meyers has spent the past three with a combat-ready unit, extending his enlistment in order to deploy to Afghanistan and the Philippines in support of Operation Enduring Freedom. His photos have appeared in *Time, Newsweek, People,* and *ESPN* magazines, and in major newspapers worldwide.

Genaro Molina

Genaro Molina has covered Pope John Paul II in Rome, AIDS in

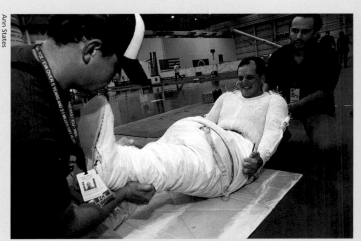

Navy Captain Michael Lopez-Alegria suits up in the Astronaut Training Wing of Houston's Johnson Space Center.

Eastern Africa, the Exxon *Valdez* oil spill, and the plight of California's migrant farm workers. His work has been exhibited at the Smithsonian Institution in Washington, D.C. He lives in Los Angeles, where he works for the *Los Angeles Times.*

Seamus Murphy

Photojournalist Seamus Murphy has broken international stories ranging from the human bone trade in Kabul, Afghanistan, to children who buy, sell, and race ponies in inner-city Dublin. Winner of World Press Photo awards in 1999 and 2001, he is represented by the Corbis Saba agency.

Captain Chuck Mussi, U.S. Air National Guard

After nearly a decade serving as a military photojournalist, Chuck Mussi left the service to pursue photography professionally. Later he attended officer candidate school and was deployed to Bosnia in 1997 as a rifle company platoon leader. He currently serves in Virginia with the National Guard Public Affairs Office.

Matthew Naythons

Matthew Naythons has spent the last 30 years as a physician, award-winning combat photographer, and book publisher. As a photographer for *Time* magazine, he covered the fall of Saigon, the Nicaraguan revolution, and the tragedy in Jonestown. He has photographed on ten *Day in the Life* projects, and is the co-producer of *A Day in the Life of the United States Armed Forces.*

Robert Nickelsberg

Robert Nickelsberg has been a contract photographer with *Time* since the early 1980s, having started his career in El Salvador. He relocated to Southeast Asia in 1986, and spent nearly 12 years based in New Delhi, India. He now lives in Brooklyn, New York.

Charles Ommanney

Charles Ommanney began his photographic career in 1991, and went on to cover the civil wars in Somalia, Rwanda, and the Sudan. In 1999 he relocated from England to the United States and became a contract photographer for *Newsweek.* He is represented by Contact Press Images, and lives in Washington, D.C.

Paolo Pellegrin

Selected to participate in the World Press Photo Master Class in 1996, Paolo Pellegrin has won a variety of awards including first prizes at the 1995 and 2000 World Press Photo awards. He is the creator of the books *Children* and *Cambodia,* and is a member of Magnum Photos.

Lucian Perkins

A staff photographer for *The Washington Post,* Lucian Perkins has covered the war in Bosnia, the Palestinian uprising in the West Bank, and the Gulf War. Among his many accolades are two Pulitzer Prizes, a World Press Photo of the Year award, and the National Press Photographers Association's Newspaper Photographer of the Year award.

Mark Peterson

Mark Peterson began taking photographs in Minneapolis in 1982, and was a United Press International photographer until 1987, when he opened the Reuters photo office in New York City. In 1991, he began working as a freelance photographer. He is represented by Corbis Saba and lives in New York City.

Larry C. Price

Winner of the 1981 Pulitzer Prize for spot news photography, and the 1985 Pulitzer Prize for feature photography for his portfolio documenting the civil wars in Angola and El Salvador, Larry Price has had his photographs published in *Time, Newsweek, GEO, U.S. News & World Report,*

National Geographic, Audubon, and other national and international publications.

Technical Sergeant Justin D. Pyle, U.S. Air Force

Justin Pyle has been working as a photographer since he was 15 years old. In his 13 years as an Air Force photographer he has documented the Kurdish plight in Northern Iraq, the conflict in Bosnia, and the Air Force Thunderbirds. He consistently wins awards in the Military Photographer of the Year competition.

Master Sergeant Keith E. Reed, U.S. Air Force

Currently assigned to Detachment 4, Air Force News Agency at Ramstein Air Base, Germany, Keith Reed has photographed military operations in more than 42 countries, and flown in and photographed more than 35 types of aircraft. A graduate of the Rochester Institute of Technology's Military Photojournalism program, Reed has published his work in major magazines including *Time* and *Newsweek.*

Alon Reininger

Alon Reininger has been involved with photojournalism since 1973. His work has won multiple awards, including a World Press Photo award in 1986, Philippe Halsman's Award for Photojournalism from the American Society of Media Photographers in 1987, and Eastman Kodak's Crystal Eagle Award in 1990. Reininger is represented by Contact Press Images and lives in Los Angeles.

Mark Richards

For more than ten years, Mark Richards' pictures have appeared in the *Communications Arts: Photography Annual.* He has covered stories from Haiti to St. Louis to Japan for a worldwide list of publications, and he is a co-founder of EP, an Internet-based group that advocates fair contracts from publishers.

Rick Rickman

The 1985 winner of the Pulitzer Prize for news photography, Rick Rickman has published photographs in *Time, Newsweek, U.S. News & World Report, People, National Geographic, Life,* and others. His photo essay on Navy SEAL training was featured in the 10th annual Visa pour l'Image international photojournalism festival in Perpignan, France. He is represented by Matrix International.

Barbara Ries

Barbara Ries has photographed for books and magazines for more than 20 years, shooting on assignment for such national

Helicopter crewmen at Naval Air Station North Island in San Diego.

Petty Officer 1st Class Tom Sperduto

Coast Guard personnel patrol the New York Harbor.

publications as *Time, Newsweek,* and *USA Today.* She has won awards from the National Press Photographers Association and the White House News Photographers' Association. She lives in the San Francisco Bay Area.

Ricki Rosen
Former *Time* magazine contract photographer Ricki Rosen has lived and worked in the Middle East since 1988. She has photographed stories on war, peace, terrorism, millennial fever, and mass immigration for book projects and international magazines including *Newsweek, People, The New York Times Magazine, Le Nouvel Observateur, L'Espresso,* and *The Sunday Times Magazine* (London).

Raul Rubiera
After studying photography at the Rochester Institute of Technology, and art at East Carolina and Florida International universities, Raul Rubiera became a staff photographer at *The Miami Herald* in 1978. He has received many awards, from the Pictures of the Year and the World Press Photo competitions, among others.

Bob Sacha
Bob Sacha is an award-winning photojournalist who splits his time between *National Geographic* and *Fortune,* where he is one of three contract photographers. He travels extensively, shooting feature stories for *Time* and travel features for *Islands.* He also contributes to many other magazines in the U.S and Europe.

Jeffery Salter
Jeffery Salter was a U.S. Navy combat cameraman from 1980 to 1985. He received special training in photojournalism at Syracuse University, and covered military exercises in Africa, South America, and Europe. Salter was twice runner-up as the National Press Photographers Association Military Photographer of the Year, and has won a World Press Photo award.

Conrad Schmidt
In 2002, Conrad Schmidt was both College and Professional Iowa Press Photographer of the Year. Attending the Eddie Adams Workshop, he won the chance to participate in *A Day in the Life of the United States Armed Forces.* He was formerly an intern at *The Dallas Morning News.*

Technical Sergeant Rick Sforza, U.S Air Force Reserves
Photo editor for the San Gabriel Valley Newspaper Group, as well as an Air Force Reserve photographer, Rick Sforza has received awards from the National Press Photographers Association and the Society of Professional Journalists, among others.

Wally Skalij
Wally Skalij began his photographic career at the *Daily Breeze* (Torrance, California) and the *San Bernardino Sun.* He has worked for the *Los Angeles Times* for the past five years, and has been honored by the California Press Photographers Association and Pictures of the Year, among others. He lives in Los Angeles.

Leif Skoogfors
An award-winning photographer and consultant in visual communications, Leif Skoogfors has made more than 20 trips to Bosnia and Eastern Europe for *Time* and *Newsweek.* His book, *The Most Natural Thing in the World,* is about the war in Northern Ireland.

Photographer's Mate 2nd Class Jennifer A. Smith, U.S. Navy
Jennifer Smith joined the Navy in 1997. After serving more than two years aboard the USS *Tarawa* in San Diego, she transferred to Fleet Combat Camera Group Pacific, traveling to places such as Australia, Hawaii, Japan, and Thailand to document military exercises and real-world events for military archives.

Petty Officer 1st Class Tom Sperduto, U.S. Coast Guard
A former Marine machine gunner and police SWAT officer, public affairs specialist Tom Sperduto discovered his love for photography after enlisting in the Coast Guard in 1998. Honors he has since received include the Alex Haley Coast Guard Photographer of the Year Award.

Ann States
A self-taught photographer with a degree in painting and drawing from the University of Georgia, Ann States has produced images for national publications for 15 years. Her work has appeared in *Business Week, People, Forbes, Newsweek, Time,* and *TV Guide.* She lives in Atlanta, Georgia.

Tom Stoddart
Tom Stoddart has covered the fall of the Berlin Wall, the buildup to the Gulf War, the siege of Sarajevo, and other significant world events. He was named Nikon Photographer of the Year in 1991 and 1992, and Nikon Feature Photographer of the Year in 2002. In 1994 and 1995 he was awarded the prestigious Visa d'Or award at the Visa pour l'Image international photojournalism festival.

Les Stone
Les Stone's photographs have been published in magazines worldwide, and he produces feature stories for many of the world's best-known publications. He has been the recipient of several World Press Photo and Pictures of the Year awards.

Jim Sugar
From 1969 to 1992, Jim Sugar was a full-time contract photographer for *National Geographic.* He has won numerous awards, including the National Press Photographers Association's Magazine Photographer of the Year in 1978. Since 1996, he has shot several stories on the U.S. military for *Popular Mechanics.* He is represented by Corbis.

Dick Swanson
Dick Swanson photographed for *Life* magazine from 1966 to 1972, covering the Vietnam War, among other topics. He has since freelanced for *Newsweek, National Geographic,* and *The Washington Post,* and has won awards from World Press Photo, the National Press Photographers Association, and the White House Press Photographer's Association, as well as the prestigious Page One Award.

Guy Tillim
Since beginning his photography career in his native South Africa in 1986, Guy Tillim has worked for international magazines and contributed to numerous

collective exhibitions at home and abroad. He was the winner of the SCAM (Societé Civile des Auteurs Multimédia) Prix Roger Pic in 2002, and was a finalist for CARE's international grand prize for humanitarian reportage in 2001.

David Turnley
Winner of the 1990 Pulitzer Prize for photography, and two World Press Picture of the Year (1988 and 1991) awards, David Turnley has photographed some of the most dramatic news events of the past 20 years in more than 75 countries. His first video work, *The Dalai Lama: At Home in Exile,* was awarded a 2000 CINE Golden Eagle award.

Peter Turnley
Based in Paris since 1978, Peter Turnley has worked in more than 85 countries, covering many of the world's major news stories. A 2000 Harvard Nieman Fellow, he has won awards from the Overseas Press Club of America and World Press Photo's Picture of the Year, among others. His photographs have appeared on the cover of *Newsweek* more than 40 times.

Commander Thomas R. Twomey, U.S. Navy
A 1983 graduate of the U.S. Naval Academy and a 1989 graduate of the Navy's "Top Gun" school, Thomas Twomey (call sign "Tumor") is currently serving as the Deputy for Joint Plans and Policy on the Staff of Commander, 3rd Fleet. His photographs appear in numerous military publications.

Ami Vitale
Ami Vitale was the National Press Photographers Association's Joseph Ehrenreich Grant recipient in 1993, and has since received many honors, including China's 1998 Humanitarian Award, and two first-place awards in the NPPA's Best of Photojournalism 2002. Vitale lives in Kashmir, and exhibited at the Open Society Institute in New York in 2002.

C. J. Walker
Although he has a degree in architecture, C. J. Walker has been a photojournalist for the past 25 years, covering stories such as Hurricane Andrew and the *Mariel* boatlift for *The Miami Herald* and *The Palm Beach Post.* He now specializes in architectural, travel, and corporate photography.

Clarence Williams
Clarence Williams was born and raised in Philadelphia, where he graduated from Temple University and interned at *The Philadelphia Tribune* and the *York Daily Record.* He began his professional career at the Times Community Newspapers in Fairfax, Virginia. Since 1994 he has worked for the *Los Angeles Times.*

Corporal Eric L. Wilson, U.S. Army
Eric Wilson has been a photographer and videographer for the Army's Training Support Center in Vilseck, Germany, for more than four years.

Donald R. Winslow
In his three-decade career as a photojournalist, writer, editor, and designer, Donald Winslow has worked as a photographer for a variety of newspapers, as well as for Reuters news service. He is the producer and co-founder of New Media for Nonprofits.

Taro Yamasaki
Taro Yamasaki started his career as a staff photographer for the *Detroit Free Press* in 1977. In 1981, he was awarded the Pulitzer Prize for feature photography. He

Taro Yamasaki

Training at the Naval Submarine Base and School in Groton, Connecticut.

became a contributing photographer for *People* in 1985, and lives in Northwestern Michigan.

Michael Yamashita
A regular contributor to the National Geographic Society since 1979, Michael Yamashita has participated in five *Day in the Life* book projects. He has won awards from the National Press Photographers Association and the Pictures of the Year Competition.

Contributors and Friends

Special thanks to our publishing partner, HarperCollins Publishers, and particularly to Jane Friedman and Cathy Hemming for their commitment to this project.

Additional special thanks to Allison Barber, Lieutenant Andrew Liggett, and all those at the Department of Defense whose cooperation and enthusiastic support helped make this book possible.

And thank you to all our advisors, contributors, and friends:

Cindy Achar
Master Sergeant William Ackerman
Marlene Adler
Lucy Albanese
Staff Sergeant Charles F. Albrecht
Commander Jeff Alderson
Roni Axelrod
Dickran Bagdassarian

Lieutenant Commander Jane Campbell
Chief Warrant Officer William Carson
Christine Caruso
Kimberly Carville
Petty Officer Megan Casey
Josephine Casey
Lieutenant Colonel Gil Castillo

The control room of the American Forces Network television studio in Frankfurt, Germany.

Mark Bailen
Captain Shane M. Balken
Oscar Ballardares
Veronica Bandrowsky
Lieutenant Colonel Stephen Barger
Ed Barker
Anna Baron
1st Lieutenant Carrie Batson
Andy Bechtolsheim
Michel Bernard
George Berndt
Richard A. Bernstein
George Bick
Deborah Bishop
Kelly Bortles
Vicki Bowker
Paul Boyce
Lieutenant Wilson Brad
Captain Tanya Bradsher
Commander Jack Brennan
Lieutenant Colonel Nicolas Britto
Chief Warrant Officer Lionel Bryant
Ed Buczek
Lisa Bullaro
Major Bob Bullock
Petty Officer Anastasia Burns
2nd Lieutenant Rosaire Bushey
Sergeant Major Keith Butler
Petty Officer Aida Cabrera-Vlasnik
Captain Don Caetano
1st Lieutenant Kelly Cahalan

Edgar Castillo
Alex Castro
Pat Cavender
Lieutenant Ann Chamberlain
Robert Cieslinski
2nd Lieutenant Jeff Clark
Victoria Clarke
Leslie Cohen
Jennifer Coley
Sergeant Major Carol Costello
Lieutenant General John Craddock
Captain Thomas Crosson
Royce-Anne Sandi Dale
Major Mark Daley
Captain Betty Annmarie Daneker
John D'Antonio
Master Sergeant Jessica D'Aurizio
Brigadier Andrew Davis
Vicki Dawes
Byron D. Day
Chief Petty Officer Marshalena Delaney
Francis J. DeMaro Jr
Larry DiRita
Arnold Drapkin
Brian Duffy
Madeleine Dwoiakowski
1st Lieutenant William Edmondson
Maureen Mahon Egen
Chief Petty Officer Eric Eggen
Rear Admiral Kevin Eldridge
Ron Elliot
Gloria Emerson

Eric Emerton
Lisa Erb
2nd Lieutenant Albert Eskalis
Michelle Faurot
Lieutenant Christian Ferguson
Doug Ferguson
Major Karen Finn
Major Paul Fitzpatrick
Technical Sergeant James Flouhouse
Major David Flynn
Andy Fontaness
Dave Foster
Carie Freimuth
1st Lieutenant Michael Friel
David Friend
Lieutenant Colonel Sarah Fry
Elena Gaiardelli
Rich Galen
Michael Garin
Admiral Ed Giambastiani
Captain Scott Gibson
Colonel Gina Giles
Andy Gilliam
Mike Gilloon
Mary Anne Golan
Major General Larry Gottardi
Rob Goza
David and Dianne Graeme-Baker
Brian Grogan
Captain Daniel Guadalupe
Anne Gunter
Joan Gustafson
Major Michael Hagen
Colonel Steve Hahn
Lieutenant Chris Haley
Major Linwood Q. Ham
Major Francisco Hamm
Lieutenant Derek Handley
Sarah Harbutt
Gary Hare
Martyn Harmon
Toni Harn

Machinery Technicians coil lines as part of training at the National Motor Lifeboat School in Ilwaco, Washington.

April and Cindy Harper
Richard Harris
Major Bill Harrison
Jess Harvey
Eileen Hawley
William Hayes
Maureen Healey-Murray
Master Sergeant Tim Helton
Matt Herron
Clare Hertel
Harriet Heyman
Master Sergeant Carlton Hill
David Holbrooke
Thomas Hopke
Major David Hsu
Christy Hudson
Elena Hughes
Mark Irion
Lieutenant Junior Grade April Isley
Captain Gina Jackson
Lieutenant Colonel M. J. Jadick
Major David Johnson
Audrey Jonckheer
Bill Joy
Peter Judd
Matt Juillerat
John Jusino

Chief Petty Officer Eugene Kachuck
Patti Kelly
Camille Kenner
Rebecca Kennerly
Lieutenant Thurraya Kent
1st Lieutenant Erin Kingsley-Smith
Françoise Kirkland
Captain Joe Kloppel
Petty Officer Jamie Knife
Jeff Korando
Sudhakar Kosaraju
Ellen Kranke
Captain Jeff Landis
Captain Don Langley
Tom LaPuzza
Bronwen Latimer
Major James Law
Steve Leiterstein
Jain Lemos
Norman Lloyd
Jay Maisel
Major Dan Maloy
Ryan Mansfield
David Manuel
Staff Sergeant George Marcec
John Markoff

In Manta, Ecuador, a U.S. Navy P-3C Orion returns from a surveillance flight in support of counter-narcotics operations.

Len Marshall
Kim Martin
Josh Marwell
Lieutenant Steven Mavica
Isabel Maxwell
Captain Thomas McCurley
Sergeant Marcus McDonald
Rich McDowell
Alfredia McGill
1st Lieutenant Herb McGill
Jim McGranachan
Lieutenant Scott McIlney
Lieutenant Commander Brendan
    McPherson
Captain Karin McWhorter
1st Lieutenant Tamara Megow
Marti Hix Mercer
Commander Kelly Merrell
Heather Miller
Dan Miller
Patricia Miller
Phillip Moffitt
Marc Monaro
Major Tomas E. Monell
Debbie Mullen
General Richard Myers
Jim Nachtwey
Susan, Mattie, and Will Naythons
Private 1st Class Benjamin Nathan
Arlene Nestel
Minh Nguyen
Rod Nordland
Jon Nylander
Margaret O'Connor
Steve Oertwig
Vince Ogilvie
Sergeant First Class Todd Oliver
Ben Orta
Barbara Owens
Perry Peltz
John Pennel
Chief Warrant Officer Steven
    Pfister
2nd Lieutenant Jessica M. Phelps
Rear Admiral Stephen Pietropaoli
Kenneth Plant
Captain Joe Plenzler
Jenny Powers
Captain Carl E. Purvis
Rear Admiral Craig Quigley

Marc Raimondi
Brigadier General Ronald Rand
Chad Raymond
Master Sergeant Chuck Reger
Jean Remley
1st Lieutenant Leticia Reyes
Beth Rickman
Laurie Rippon
Jeffrey H. Roberts
Dick Robertson
Gunnery Sergeant Gideon Rogers
Jerry Rosenberg
Philip Rosi
Katherine Ball Ross
Petty Officer Paul Roszkowski
Galen and Barbara Rowell
Sergeant 1st Class Melanie Rowton
Patrick Rozmajzl
Bert Rudman
Technical Sergeant Jose Ruiz
Kathy Ryan
Lieutenant Colonel William
    Rynecki
Marcel Saba
Barbara Sadick
David Sanders
Doug Sayers
Helen Segale
Doug Sheldon
Goksun Sipahioglu
Douglas Smith
Captain Sheldon Smith
Captain Joseph Smith
Tracy Smith
Chief Petty Officer Daniel
    Smithymand
Commander William Spann
Juan Spencer
Major Lesa Spivey
Phyllis Springer
Lynn Staley
Major Sandra Steinberg
Lieutenant Kevin Stephens
Michelle Stephenson
Dick Stipe
Liz Stone
Eric Strauss
David Strettell
Phillip Stroub
Sergeant 1st Class B. Sutton

Maria Taylor
Captain James Taylor
Major Cynthia Teramae
Commander M. C. Tevelson
Judith Thurman
Captain Joe Trechter
Jonathan Trumble
George Ulrichs
Terry Vandan-Heuvel
Technical Sergeant Guy Volb
John Wallach
Lois Walsh
Christine Walsh
Captain Edwina Walton
Lieutenant Christopher Watt
Megan Weaver
Technical Sergeant Donald Weber
Susan Weinberg
Cap Weinberger
Maureen Welch
Commander David Wells
Peter West
Kevin Westberg
Roger Wetherell
Jerry Whitaker
Captain Jill Whitesell
Joy Whitmore
2nd Lieutenant Tony Wickman
Technical Sergeant Karin Wickwire
Preston Williams
Brad Wilson
Gail Winston
David Wolfson
Lieutenant Jeff Wood
Captain Mark Wooster
1st Lieutenant Karim Wright
Chief Warrant Officer Rob Wyman
Chuck Yeager
Jon Yoshishige
Commander Jacqueline Yost
Bill Youngberg
Lieutenant Commander Ed Zeigler
David Zimmerman
Mort Zuckerman

Special thanks to David Cohen
and Rick Smolan, who were
available to HarperCollins
Publishers as consultants on
this project.

Remembrance

Blake Wallens was married to my daughter, Raina. Blake grew up in California; long before he married Raina, Blake adopted my wife, Sharon, our son, Eric, and me as his East Coast family. And Blake became our second son.

On September 11, 2001, Blake, at age 31, was killed, along with nearly 3,000 others, in the attack on the World Trade Center. His radiant young life was cut short at a moment when he had everything to live for, and so much yet to give.

A Day in the Life of the United States Armed Forces, with gratitude steeped in sorrow, is in memory of Blake and for the men and women who perished with him on September 11th. Our gratitude is for all that they were; our sorrow is for all that was yet to come.

They will be with us as long as there is memory.

Lewis J. Korman
Producer, A Day in the Life of the
    United States Armed Forces
October 22, 2002

Matthew Blake Wallens
April 16, 1970–September 11, 2001

Staff Sergeant Gary L. Kieffer

U.S. Army soldiers partner with the New York Police Department on security patrols in Grand Central Station.

255

Project Team

Project Producers
Matthew Naythons
Lewis J. Korman

Editorial Director
Dawn Sheggeby

Director of Photography
Acey Harper

Design Director
Tom Walker

Executive Producer
David Hume Kennerly

Assistant Editor, Website Director
Jennifer Castle

Assistant Director of Photography
Shonquis Moreno

Photography Logistics Director
Peter Goggin

Project Assistants
Angela Martenez
Heather McNama

Assignment Editors
Guy Cooper
Peter Goggin
Staff Sergeant Gary Kieffer
Florence Nash
Travis Ruse

Special Advisor
General (Ret.) Wesley K. Clark

**Department of Defense
Project Officer**
Lieutenant Andrew G. Liggett

Picture Editors
James A. Colton, *Sports Illustrated*
Maura Foley, *People*
Nik Kleinberg, *ESPN Magazine*
Susan Mettler, *Forbes*
Michelle Molloy, *Newsweek*
Jodi Peckman, *Rolling Stone*

Design Assistant
Wayne Kogan

Logo Design
Adrian Pulfer, *A/3 Design*

Website Design
Scott Abbott, *Marker Seven*

Marketing Consultant
John Silbersack

Video Producer
Mike Cerre

Special Editorial Operations
Spencer Reiss

Caption Writers
Jim Calio
Alex Castle
Wendy Marech
Shonquis Moreno

Caption Researchers
Bryan Carmel
Scott Prendergast

Copy Editors
Magdalen Powers
Kate Warne

Video Consultant
Marjorie Lipton

EpiCom Media
Lewis J. Korman
Robert Gottlieb
Matthew Naythons
John Silbersack
Shelley Schultz

Executive Assistant to Producer
Virginia Castanon

Accountants
Mark Imowitz, *Imowitz,
Koenig and Co., LLP*

Legal Advisors
Richard Heller,
Juliana O'Niell,
Helen Wan,
Frankfurt Kurnit Klein & Selz

Public Relations
Cathy Saypol, *CSPR, Inc.*

The Naval Base Exchange at the Norfolk Naval Station in Virginia.

Color Separations
North Market Street Graphics,
Philadelphia

Color Transparency Processing
U.S. Color Lab, New York

Digital Photo Editing
Photo Mechanic software
from Camera Bits

Marines in Okinawa take part in a live-fire jungle training exercise.